❀ Northland Wildflowers

Revised Edition

Northland

John B. Moyle & Evelyn W. Moyle

Wildflowers

The Comprehensive Guide to the Minnesota Region

New Photography by

John Gregor
ColdSnap Photography

University of Minnesota Press
Minneapolis • London

Published by the University of Minnesota Press
111 Third Avenue South, Suite 290
Minneapolis, MN 55401-2520
http://www.upress.umn.edu

Library of Congress Cataloging-in-Publication Data
Moyle, John B. (John Briggs), 1909–1977.
    Northland wildflowers : the comprehensive guide to the Minnesota region /
John B. Moyle and Evelyn W. Moyle ; new photography by John Gregor.—Rev. ed.
        p.   cm.
Includes bibliographical references (p.   ) and index.
    ISBN 0-8166-3571-4 (HC : acid-free paper)
    ISBN 0-8166-3572-2 (PB : acid-free paper)
1. Wild flowers—Minnesota—Identification. 2. Wild flowers—Minnesota—Pictorial works.
I. Moyle, Evelyn W.   II. Moyle, John B. (John Briggs), 1909–1977. Northland wild flowers.
III. Title.
    QK168 .M73 2001
    582.13'09776—dc21   00–010347

Printed in China by HK Scanner Arts Int'l Ltd
Book design by Diane Gleba Hall

The University of Minnesota is an equal-opportunity educator and employer.

11 10 09 08 07 06 05 04 03 02 01   10 9 8 7 6 5 4 3 2 1

To Walter John Moyle, horticulturist, and

Carl Otto Rosendahl, botanist and teacher,

both of whom knew and enjoyed the wildflowers,

and to all who are helping preserve our

wildflower heritage

❀ Contents

❀ *Preface*

NORTHLAND WILDFLOWERS was written for those who enjoy Minnesota's wild-flowers and would like to know more about them. Although it primarily describes species found in Minnesota, it will also be useful to people in adjacent states since plants recognize no such boundaries. We hope the book will benefit both the reader and the wildflowers. Wildflowers are an important part of our natural and cultural heritage—a heritage that provides much outdoor enjoyment and needs our under-standing and help for preservation in the future.

This edition of *Northland Wildflowers* has been revised to include new photogra-phy by John Gregor of ColdSnap Photography. The book has also been reorganized by color of bloom, which, along with the new photographs, will make the book much easier to use. Several new species have been added, many of which were suggested over the years by readers. As before, botanical terminology has been kept to a minimum.

Northland Wildflowers is based on John Moyle's expertise in botany and in writ-ing. John grew up in a nursery owned and operated by his father as a family business in which everyone was expected to help out. His grandfather was a preacher, so the written and spoken word were important in the production of catalogs, sales pitches, and sermons. John continued his education at the University of Minnesota, where he earned his Ph.D. in botany. During his career with the Minnesota Department of Natural Resources, he wrote and published many popular and scientific articles and was a frequent contributor to *The Minnesota Volunteer*. His work required extensive travel throughout the state, and he made note of where wildflowers grew and when they bloomed.

A year or so after John's retirement, we started work on the first edition of *Northland Wildflowers* and traveled throughout the state, notebooks and camera in hand. John made the final identifications and did the writing, while I took most of the photographs and typed and edited the manuscript. All this time, John was suffering from cancer but hesitated to take pain medication from fear of diminishing his ability to think and write. He lived long enough to hold the book in his hand and to know it would be a success.

John and I are grateful to many wildflower enthusiasts for suggestions, encouragement, companionship afield, and friendly advice both botanical and photographic. We wish especially to thank Mr. John McKane, Dr. John W. Moore, Dr. and Mrs. Lloyd Smith Jr., Dr. Walter Breckenridge, Mr. and Mrs. Ralph Forester, Mr. John Dobie, Mr. Rupert Lowrey, Dr. Max Partch, Mr. William Longley, Dr. and Mrs. Ed Rogier, Dr. Robert Bergad, and Dr. Tom and Carol Waters.

I am also grateful to our son Peter Moyle and our daughter Susan Studlar for their help and advice, and to our son Joseph Moyle and our daughter Virginia Pezalla for their interest and encouragement on this revised edition. Welby Smith generously offered his assistance with updating of botanical information and with verifying the accuracy of the photographs. I also wish to thank Todd Orjala, my editor at the University of Minnesota Press, and John Gregor for contributing his beautiful photography to this edition of the book and for his help with reorganizing the book.

EVELYN W. MOYLE

🌸 *Photographer's Acknowledgments*

WHEN I WAS IN THE FIELD working and someone would ask me what I was doing (I was quite conspicuous with a backpack full of camera gear, several cameras, lenses, tripods, and lighting scrims), I would tell them I was rephotographing *Northland Wildflowers*. More often than not they would then reach into their day pack and produce a well-worn copy of the book. After this happened several times, I knew that I was working on what is considered by many to be a classic guidebook for our region.

I was given one season to complete the assignment of photographing all the portraits for this book—a daunting task, and one that I soon realized was a labor of love. We (the ColdSnap studio) managed to produce over 220 of the wildflower portraits reproduced in this text. Several of our images could not replace the classic images from the first book photographed by Evelyn Moyle. Those images are reproduced using new print technology in this text.

I would like first to thank Evelyn Moyle for allowing me to participate in this project. I have had the honor of spending many hours with her, both in the field and in front of a computer or light table.

My wife, Jenny Gregor, contributed to this book in many ways. Several of the photographs are by her, and she frequently assisted me in the field, helping me find, identify, and photograph most of the rest of the portrait photographs. In addition to being my wife, she is my business partner and best friend.

Randy Hagar and Mark Lissick work with me in the studio. They helped field outings and several of the portrait photographs are by them (these are noted with individual photo credits). Randy and Mark also held down the fort when I was away on my many field trips.

Bob Djupstrom and Kelly Randall from the Minnesota Department of Natural Resources (DNR), Scientific and Natural Areas, gave me invaluable assistance, guiding me to various sites and times for catching flower blooms. Welby Smith reviewed my work for accuracy and offered constructive criticism and encouragement. The citizens of Minnesota are lucky to have the DNR, a valuable resource staffed with competent, friendly professionals.

I would like to thank the following photographers who helped us fill in the gaps: Rick Haug, Bill Johnson, Welby Smith, Cole Burrell, and David Cavagnaro. One final person who deserves special mention is Dennis Hageman, who has helped me understand some of the secrets that the prairie holds.

To the countless people I met on the trail or in the field who offered me information and encouragement, I express my gratitude. I hope I run into you again, with your brand-new copy of *Northland Wildflowers*.

JOHN GREGOR
ColdSnap Photography

🌸 *Introduction*

With a hi ho
  And a hey nonny nonny
And the Northland flowers
  Spring so bonny

AND SO IT IS in the Northland that is Minnesota and the adjacent landscapes. Winter may be long and cold, but with spring come the wildflowers that brighten the countryside until the frosts of autumn. There are many kinds of wildflowers, and they grow in many places.

Of the 1,700 species of flowering plants that are wild in Minnesota, about one-quarter can be considered wildflowers. Wildflowers are easily recognized but as a group are difficult to define. Whether a wild plant is a wildflower depends on its appearance, where it grows, and who sees it. It could be a wildflower, a weed, or just a bit of natural greenery, depending on one's point of view. Generally we have selected herbs with colorful or otherwise interesting flowers for inclusion in this book. Some have or have had practical uses, some have interesting historical connections, but most are just colorful wildflowers.

Wildflowers are for seeing, but primarily for seeing by insects. Like many birds and like us, insects have color vision. The color of wildflowers, as well as their odor and nectar, attracts insects and encourages them to visit and pollinate flowers, often those of a particular type. Watch a bee or some other insect working on flowers. Usually it does not visit flowers at random but rather goes from flower to flower of the same kind. The varied shapes and color patterns of wildflowers, some of which, like the lady's-slippers, are marvelously complex, are stratagems by which cross-pollination is made more certain. By cross-pollination the genetic inheritance of a plant is maintained, reshuffled, and renewed. During their long history, plants and insects have developed together to their mutual benefit.

Wildflowers also should be studied for the satisfaction that comes with understanding. Flowers and fruits provide the keys to natural relationships of plants and for the most part are the characteristics by which plants can be grouped into families and genera. Understanding these relationships of the more than 250,000 flowering plants of this green world is one of the great achievements of the human mind and is a cornerstone of natural science.

In a broad developmental sense wildflowers are as successful as we are—they are here. In the long history of survival each has developed variations on the general life forms and processes, including the biochemical. Each produces many kinds of chemical compounds. Some have been useful to us as drugs (quinine and digitalis are examples) or for other purposes. From a practical viewpoint alone, we should take care not to lose the wild plants that can produce complex substances whose value is as yet unknown but which we may sometime need.

Plant Names

Wildflowers and other plants have two kinds of names: common and botanical. The common names for the wildflowers included here are those most generally used and accepted in this region. Usually they are the names recognized in botanical manuals, guides, and checklists. Often, however, a wildflower has several common names, and sometimes several wildflowers share the same common name. In some cases, especially for uncommon kinds of plants, the common name is an obvious translation of the botanical name.

Botanical names, which consist of two Latin or Latinized words, have the advantage of being accepted by botanists worldwide. Theoretically there is only one correct botanical name for a species of plant. This is the first published botanical name correctly assigned to it. However, synonyms often exist and sometimes persist, reflecting differences of opinion among botanists, and technicalities that cannot be considered here.

The first word of the botanical name is the genus, or general group, to which a particular kind or species of plant belongs. The generic names are always capitalized. The second word designates the species and is the specific name. For example, the botanical name of the Smooth Wild Rose is *Rosa* (Latin for "rose") *blanda* (Latin for "smooth"). Botanical names used in this book agree, for the most part, with those in *Vascular Plants of Minnesota: A Checklist and Atlas* by G. B. Ownbey and T. Morley (1991) and with H. Gleason and A. Cronquist's *Manual of Vascular Plants of Northeastern United States and Adjacent Canada* (2d ed., 1991). Synonyms, original authors of the names, and related details can be found in these more technical books. Other botanical works dealing with the names and ranges of plants have also been consulted.

Plant names, both common and botanical, often have interesting histories and may or may not describe the plant to which they are assigned. Linnaeus and other early botanists who gave botanical names to many of our plants were interested primarily in assigning distinctive names that were not in general use. For example, *Zizania*, the generic name of Wild Rice, was borrowed from *zizanion*, the Greek word for the "tares" in New Testament parables. It is a distinctive name, but it does not describe Wild Rice. Other nomenclatural oddities, some mentioned in the text, include names borrowed from ancient mythology. *Heracleum* from Herakles and *Circaea* from Circe are examples.

Latin, it should be remembered, with a considerable borrowing from Greek, was once the language of science. Linnaeus (1707–78) and those who followed him tried to describe each species of plant in a few Latin words and then selected two descriptive or distinctive words as the botanical name. This is the "binomial system."

In addition to the generic and specific names, "varieties" marking minor differences within a species may have Latin names. An example is our common variety of Canada Violet, *Viola canadensis* var. *rugulosa*.

What Is a Flower?

It is generally accepted by botanists that a flower is a short stem or shoot, bearing several kinds of leaves modified to aid cross-pollination and the production of seeds. The floral leaves are of four kinds. Starting from the outside, they are sepals (forming the calyx), petals (forming the corolla), stamens, which produce pollen, and the pistil or pistils, which enclose ovules and later the seeds. The more primitive flowers have conspicuous flower parts (petals and sometimes sepals) that are free (not joined together) and somewhat leaf- or paddle-shaped. In contrast, the more highly developed flowers have petals that are joined, at least at the base, and are often modified in shape or structure. Some kinds of plants have flower adaptations to facilitate pollination by wind and even water. Meadow Rue and Wild Rice are examples of wind-pollinated flowers.

The color of flowers is an obvious characteristic and a starting point for the appreciation of wildflowers. However, color is so variable, sometimes even within a single species, that the use of color as a basis for identification has to be done with care. Species with yellow or pure white flowers are fairly constant, but nearly all other colored species occasionally have white (albino) flowers. These sometimes cross with the normal type to give intermediate shades. Most multicolored garden flowers originated in this way. Some kinds of wildflowers change color as they age. Examples are Large-flowered Trillium, which turns from white to pink, and the Virginia Bluebell,

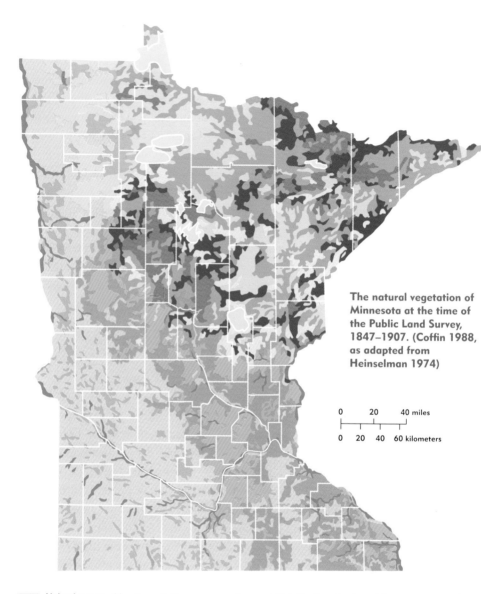

The natural vegetation of
Minnesota at the time of
the Public Land Survey,
1847–1907. (Coffin 1988,
as adapted from
Heinselman 1974)

0   20   40 miles

0   20   40   60 kilometers

Upland prairie—bluestems, Indian grass, needle
and grama grasses; composites and other forbs

Prairie wetland—blue-joint grass, cord grass,
cattails, rushes, sedges

Aspen parkland—aspen groves with prairie and
sedge meadow openings

Oak woodland and brushland—bur oak and pin oak,
aspen and hazel thickets, and prairie openings

Floodplain forest—silver maple, elm, cottonwood,
willow

Maple-basswood forest—elm, basswood,
sugar maple, red oak, white oak

Northern hardwood forest—sugar maple,
yellow birch, basswood, and occasional
white pine

Great Lakes pine forest—white pine,
red pine with paper birch and aspen

Jack pine forest—jack pine with red pine,
oak and hazel

Boreal hardwood-conifer forest—aspen,
birch, balsam fir, white spruce, white cedar

Peatland—sedge fen, black spruce–sphagnum
bog, white cedar–black ash swamp

4

which is pink in bud but blue in full flower. The color photographs show the most usual color to the extent that it has been possible to reproduce it.

Arrangement of Plants in This Book

Despite the difficulties in using color to identify flowers, it is the characteristic that most people notice first. Flowers in this book have therefore been grouped by color, and within each color section by family. Neither of these characteristics is exact. Color is variable, as noted earlier, and may be hard to determine, as when pink shades into lavender, blue into purple, or red into maroon or brown. A flower may also be of two or more colors, in which case the color most conspicuous from a short distance has been chosen for placement. For example, a flower with two blue petals and one white petal will be found in the blue section, a white flower with pink stripes may be in the pink section if the pink seems to predominate. Flower color may vary with location. If a flower cannot be found in one color section, check the next most likely color, noting also the season and place of growth. For example, Rue Anemones are generally pink in the Twin Cities area but are often white elsewhere. Since white is the most prevalent color in Minnesota, Rue Anemone is found in the white section of the book.

Where to Find Wildflowers

Minnesota is a fine place to see and enjoy wildflowers. It is a botanical crossroads where three major vegetation types meet: the southern and eastern hardwood forests; the northern forests of pines, spruces, and other evergreens; and the western tallgrass prairies. Within these general vegetation types are many habitats characterized by specific groups of wildflowers and other plants. The more extensive of these are the central sandplain extending northward from Anoka to Brainerd; the much eroded limestone and sandstone country of the southeast; the rocky Lake Superior coast; the many bogs, marshes, and muskegs of the north, including the vast Red Lake Peatland; the scenic St. Croix and lower Mississippi River valleys; and the rocky prairies of the extreme southwestern counties.

Original boundaries of major vegetation types have been much modified by human activities such as farming, lumbering, and suppression of wildfires. But here and there remnants of the original vegetation can be found in forests, parks, and wild-life areas and along rights-of-way and watercourses. Often it is the boundary transition areas, or "edges," of vegetation types that are most favorable for wildflowers. Habitat disturbance, natural or man-made, favors many kinds of wild plants. Examples of such disturbed areas are river bottoms flooded in early spring, sites of recent forest or prairie fires, and recently graded or brushed roadsides where herbicides have not been used extensively. To be successful, native plants with conspicuous flowers must grow where they can be seen easily and are available to insects. Areas of long-established vegetation, such as dense mature woods, sedge-covered marshes, and thick stands of tall prairie grasses, often have fewer conspicuous wildflowers than do more open places.

Most wildflowers of European origin thrive best along roads and in old fields, pastures, and waste corners where the habitat has been modified by humans and domestic animals. These plants have long lived with humans and have been unwittingly selected by them during the long history of agriculture.

For finding wildflowers, a good highway map is most helpful. The Minnesota Department of Transportation publishes maps showing where wildflowers have been planted along highways as well as the location of state parks, larger state and federal wildlife management areas, and public forest lands. Where railroad and highway rights-of-way run side by side, there is often a strip of wildland that has never been broken, where native wildflowers remain and thrive.

Another resource is an excellent publication by the Minnesota Department of Natural Resources (DNR), *A Guide to Minnesota's Scientific and Natural Areas*, which contains maps showing the location of well over a hundred undisturbed plant and animal communities, which vary with the land (e.g., virgin prairie, old-growth forest, peatlands, and others) and are now protected by the state. A special effort is being made to protect land where rare and endangered species exist and to care for it so the species endure.

The Minnesota Chapter of The Nature Conservancy is also active in preserving

Roadside plantings along U.S. Highway 52 in Dakota County

Controlled burn at Gneiss Outcrops Scientific and Natural Area in southwestern Minnesota

natural communities. It publishes a guide containing maps and a history of its preserves, some of which it manages in conjunction with the DNR or has helped the state acquire. The DNR, through its County Biological Survey Program, also publishes large-scale county maps showing the location of Natural Communities and Rare Species. Atlases of county maps drawn to a larger scale than the usual highway maps are also available at booksellers, often as fishing and hunting guides. They show smaller roads, minor geographic features, and railroads.

On the public lands of Minnesota and adjacent states and provinces wildflowers can be seen, enjoyed, and photographed, but they should not be picked, transplanted, or trampled. Not only are these activities unwise and ecologically unsound, they are often illegal.

The sections that follow describe areas we have favored for wildflower viewing. Most are state parks, because they contain some of the oldest protected areas in the state, have good hiking trails, and often have a naturalist in residence. Guides to the many natural areas that are being preserved throughout the state are generally kept up to date and are increasingly useful as unprotected wildflower habitat disappears. Guides to these areas include:

Minnesota Department of Natural Resources. 1999. *A Guide to Minnesota's Scientific and Natural Areas.* Section of Wildlife, Scientific and Natural Areas Program, Minnesota Department of Natural Resources, St. Paul.

Minnesota Native Plant Society. 1996. *Minnesota Native Plant Society's Guide to Spring Wildflowers: Twin Cities Region*. Minnesota Native Plant Society, University of Minnesota, St. Paul.

The Nature Conservancy. 1994. *The Guide to The Nature Conservancy Preserves in Minnesota*. The Nature Conservancy, Minnesota Chapter, Minneapolis.

Twin Cities Area

One can see and enjoy wildflowers in several excellent spots in the Twin Cities area.

The Eloise Butler Wildflower and Bird Sanctuary, founded by and named after a Minneapolis schoolteacher, is part of the Minneapolis park system and is located near the western edge of the city. Here woodland, marsh, and prairie flowers, many identified with markers, can be seen from well-kept walking trails. A naturalist is on duty, and public facilities are available.

Minnehaha Park, especially along Minnehaha Creek below the falls, has interesting spring wildflowers. Here in seepage areas Skunk Cabbage blooms soon after the snow melts. Forget-me-not and Yellow Flag appear later.

The University of Minnesota Landscape Arboretum near Chanhassen has fine trails through deciduous forest and prairie. A wide boardwalk crosses a bog, and naturalistic plantings of some of the less common wildflowers can be seen. Many shrubs, trees, vines, and garden plants are planted along several miles of winding roads. The beautiful headquarters building has a botanical library.

Wolsfeld Woods Scientific and Natural Area near Wayzata is a remnant of the Big Woods, which once covered much of central Minnesota. It is a fine place to see early spring wildflowers.

Carver Park Reserve, near Victoria, west of Lake Minnetonka, is one of several managed by Hennepin County Parks. Along its

Big Woods forest, which once covered much of southeastern Minnesota, including portions of the Twin Cities

walking trails through woodlands, upland open areas, and swamps are many common wildflowers. Those who enjoy nature little modified find this an especially good hiking area. Many autumn composites—asters, goldenrod, and bonesets—grow here in the open areas. It is also a good spot for seeing water birds, including the rare trumpeter swans. In the fine headquarters building a naturalist can direct you to museum displays and educational programs as well as to the best places to find wildflowers in bloom.

Southeastern Minnesota

In the hilly country of the southeast, many of the most easily reached wildflower areas are literally "down in the valley." These valleys were wooded at the time of settlement and remain so. They have an abundance of spring wildflowers. Dry southwest-facing slopes on hills and bluffs, especially along the Mississippi River, are characterized by prairie plants. Such slopes are locally called "goat prairies." Most of the level uplands are intensely farmed. Only a few of the wildflower spots of the southeast can be mentioned here.

Frontenac State Park stands on the edge of the Mississippi River valley and high above Lake Pepin. Although primarily a historic site, there are wooded trails, some of

them steep, along which grow many kinds of wildflowers and ferns. State Highway 242 from Red Wing to the park follows an ancient valley containing woods and long swamps full of marsh vegetation. One of these marshes is within the park.

Of the several state parks farther south, our choices for spring wildflower enjoyment are Carley, south of Plainview; Forestville, near Preston; and Lake Louise, near the Iowa border at Le Roy. All include river bottoms in which grow wildflowers such as False Rue Anemone, Virginia Bluebell, Swamp Buttercup, Dutchman's Breeches, White Trout Lily, and Spring Beauty. In spring the borders of streams, many of them trout streams, are carpeted with the blue flowers and mint-scented vines of Ground Ivy. Originally from Eurasia this plant is now unwelcome, as it may displace native plants.

Mesic prairie landscape at Schaefer Prairie in McLeod County

In backwaters, old channels, and oxbow lakes of the Mississippi River are extensive stands of American Lotus Lily and Arrowhead. Partridge Pea and Flowering Spurge grow along roads. Near Northfield is Nerstrand Big Woods State Park, a rolling, upland, wooded area with streams and a waterfall. Wildflowers here are representative of the Big Woods, a forest of sugar maple, basswood, and other broad-leaved trees that once covered much of south-central Minnesota. The fine display of spring wildflowers includes the rare and endangered Minnesota Trout Lily, Minnesota's only endemic species of wildflower. Marsh Marigold grows in wetter areas.

Southern and Southwestern Minnesota

This area, now generally fertile farmland, was once prairie, except for the wooded stream and lake margins protected from prairie fires. Wildflower areas are now limited mostly to state parks, wildlife areas, and trails, and along rights-of-way, especially where highways and railroads are side by side. Often parks have preserved woods rather than prairie. The steep wooded lands in stream valleys were less suitable for farming than the prairies and were early valued as picnic spots by the prairie pioneers.

Minneopa State Park near Mankato and Kilen Woods near Windom are examples of wooded valleys in prairie country. Both have trails along which are many wildflowers, especially in spring. At Minneopa there is a beautiful waterfall.

For typical prairie vegetation and wildflowers, we suggest the rocky country of Rock and Pipestone Counties in the extreme southwest. Blue Mounds State Park has a fine display of Prickly Pear, which blooms about the first week in July. The park is also home to the only Minnesota herd of bison. At Pipestone National Monument a self-guiding nature trail provides names of many of the prairie plants. Here also are the historic pipestone quarries and an interesting museum emphasizing the history of the Native Americans who first used them.

Farther north, typical prairie vegetation of morainic areas can be seen at Lac Qui Parle State Park and the adjacent wildlife area, and at Big Stone Lake State Park. Big Stone Lake also provides a beautiful view of the hills of South Dakota. At Glacial Lakes State Park and along Glacial Lakes State Trail, which leads to it, are many views of hilly prairie. The highway between Terrace and Sunberg is especially scenic, with rolling hills and scattered small lakes and potholes. Many late summer and autumn wildflowers, such as blazing stars, sunflowers, goldenrods, and asters, thrive here. Here also can be seen such native legumes as the Prairie Plum (*Astragalus crassicarpus*), with its low clusters of purple flowers in early spring, and the Prairie Turnip (*Pediomelum esculentum*), whose roots were a food of the Dakota Indians.

East-Central Minnesota

North of the Twin Cities and covering much of the area between the Mississippi and St. Croix Rivers is a sandy plain laid down and leveled by the meandering Mississippi at the end of the last Ice Age. Here is much prairie vegetation, and where there have

North Shore of Lake Superior at the mouth of the Fall River near Grand Marais

been no recent intense prairie fires, thin stands of oak (oak savanna) and aspen forest. Because the soil is sandy, vegetation is less dense than on the clayey prairies farther west. In late spring it is often gardenlike with a variety of bright flowers. Here can be seen Carolina Puccoon, Butterflyweed—both bright orange—Downy Phlox, Western and Bracted Spiderwort, Large-flowered Penstemon, Pansy Violet, and Purple Avens. A good time to visit the sandplain is between June 1 and July 1.

Within this general area are the Mille Lacs Wildlife Area, near Onamia, the Sherburne National Wildlife Refuge, near Princeton, and Sand Dunes State Forest, near Zimmerman. At the last park, on old sand dunes and blowouts are found the plants that pioneer such unstable areas.

Near Onamia are several shallow wild rice lakes, such as Lake Onamia along U.S. Highway 169, which have long been harvested by Native Americans. Mille Lacs Kathio State Park has both forest and open areas with representative wildflowers. Along the west shore of Mille Lacs Lake is one of the best spots in Minnesota to see Large-flowered Trillium, which blooms in spring. When in this area, do not miss the Mille Lacs Indian Museum operated by the Minnesota Historical Society. It is across the highway from Grand Casino on the shore of Mille Lacs Lake. Of special interest here are its fine displays of Native American uses of wild plants.

East of the sandplain is the St. Croix River valley, with its rocky bluffs. Spring wildflowers are common in wooded areas along State Highway 95 running from Stillwater to Interstate State Park at Taylors Falls. The latter location is near the northern limit of several kinds of southern and eastern wildflowers. On river bottoms is an open forest that is flooded each spring. Here in summer you can find Cardinal Flower and False Dragonhead. Summer wildflowers also flourish along State Highway 95.

Northeastern Minnesota
Duluth, on the southern edge of the northeastern Arrowhead Country, can be a base for several wildflower expeditions. Its well-planned system of city parks includes many wooded areas and ravines. Skyline Parkway traverses rocky areas high above the city. Minnesota Point, a long sandy spit extending into Lake Superior and enclosing the harbor, is well worth visiting. In the city park near the end of the point are plants typical of sandy Lake Superior beaches. Here Beach Pea is abundant. Jay Cooke State Park, a short drive from Duluth, contains a spectacular gorge along the St. Louis River. In spring there is the added attraction of the abundant and decorative Large-flowered Trillium.

Lake Superior somewhat moderates the climate along its coast, and along the North Shore several kinds of wildflowers may be seen that are less common or rare elsewhere in the state. Typical are Flowering Raspberry, with its spreading white

Stemless lady's-slippers (*Cypripedium acaule*) in a bog in the Chippewa National Forest

flowers and maple-like leaves, and Tall Lungwort (locally called Bluebell). The latter has nodding blue flowers and is a close relative of the Virginia Bluebell found in the southeast. Several European plants thrive here as wildflowers. Orange Hawkweed makes bright orange patches along roads and in clearings. Scentless Chamomile, Tansy, Common St. John's-wort, and Ox-eye Daisy all occur along roads. In some places plantings of Bird's-foot Trefoil and Crown Vetch in road cuts provide bright yellow and pink patches.

Split Rock Lighthouse State Park is an interesting place to stop. In addition to the marvelous view, one can see rock plants such as Harebell, Three-toothed Cinquefoil, and Shrubby Cinquefoil. Growth of orange lichens on the rocks here is promoted by the droppings of gulls. Farther up the shore is Caribou Falls State Wayside Park. The trail, somewhat difficult to negotiate at its upper end, leads to one of Minnesota's most beautiful waterfalls. Along the trail are many of the characteristic forest plants and wildflowers of the region.

Inland in the Superior National Forest and the state forests are many stopping and camping places. The Boundary Waters Canoe Area Wilderness and Isle Royale National Park in Lake Superior are good choices for an extended holiday. The latter can be reached by boat from Grand Portage. *Canoe Country Flora* by Mark Stensaas (1996) is a guide to the plants and trees of the Boundary Waters.

North-Central Minnesota

Much of this rolling forested country was originally covered with white and red pine that fell under the logger's axe, but scattered stands of magnificent pine remain, especially in Cass, Itasca, and Hubbard Counties. Here such typical northern forest plants as Large-leaved Aster, Lindley's Aster, and Wild Sarsaparilla are abundant. Fireweed and Pearly Everlasting are common in old fields and openings, and Ox-eye Daisy and Tall Buttercup grow along open roadsides and in pastures.

There are many grassy and mossy bogs and marshes. Such oddities as Pitcher Plant and Sundew (both insectivorous), a variety of shrubs of the heath family, and some low plants that range northward into subarctic and arctic regions grow in these habitats. Remember that bogs and "muskegs" (as the wooded bogs are called) are hard going. They can be dangerous and are the homes of myriad mosquitoes. Those who wish to see some of the bog plants without too great an effort might try Dr. Robert's Nature Trail near Douglas Lodge in Itasca State Park.

Northwestern Minnesota

Few lakes are found in extreme western and northwestern Minnesota. Much of this area is within the basin of a very large ancient lake—Glacial Lake Agassiz—that was impounded and then drained naturally at the end of the last Ice Age. Here are the Red Lake peatland, or "Big Bog," and the Red Lake Indian Reservation, and in the Red River valley much level farmland that was originally low prairie. An interesting trip

Tamarack bog typical of many peatland areas of northern Minnesota

through a vast area of level peatland could start at Redby or Red Lake on Lower Red Lake. Follow the Great River Road (Highways 1 and 89) to the Agassiz National Wildlife Refuge and the Thief Lake Wildlife Area. Moose and many kinds of water-fowl are found here as well as an abundance of marsh plants and summer and autumn wildflowers.

In the Red River valley the main highways and the railroads that usually parallel them often run in a north-south direction. They follow the ancient beach lines of Glacial Lake Agassiz, and abundant and diverse prairie wildflowers often grow on the sandy and gravelly soil of these beaches. Toward the southern end of this ancient lake basin near Moorhead is Buffalo River State Park, in which many kinds of prairie plants can be seen, including White Lady's-slipper in early summer. Eastward, near Detroit Lakes, are many Wild Rice stands; some of the most accessible are in the Tamarac National Wildlife Refuge. Wild Rice is hand harvested here about September 1.

Wildflowers and the Calendar

In Minnesota some wildflowers are in bloom throughout the growing season. However, most can be grouped, somewhat arbitrarily, into spring, summer, and autumn flowering kinds. These floral seasons correspond only approximately to the calendar seasons, and for the Twin Cities region can be dated about as follows:

Spring, from about April 15 to June 15, with a peak around May 15. Among the first spring wildflowers to bloom are Skunk Cabbage, Hepatica, Pasque Flower, and Bloodroot.

Summer, from about June 16 to August 15, with a peak bloom around July 15. Typical of this period are Butterflyweed, Indian Paint Brush, Brown-eyed Susan, Ox-eye Daisy, Grayheaded Coneflower, and Prairie Clover.

Autumn, from about August 16 to killing frost (usually around October 5), with a peak bloom about September 10. Characteristic of the autumn blooming season are asters, goldenrods, blazing stars, sunflowers, Joe-Pye Weed, and gentians.

Minnesota is about 400 miles long from south to north. Spring usually comes 4 or 5 days earlier in the southeast than in the Twin Cities area. The last killing frost of spring may be expected about a week later along Lake Superior than in the Twin Cities area and 3 to 4 weeks later in the Boundary Waters Canoe Area Wilderness. The growing season is about 160 days in the extreme southeast, 155 days in the Twin Cities area, and 100 days or even less along the northern border. The onset of spring, as shown by observations of plant development, varies considerably in different years and for different kinds of plants. Spring development of some common kinds of forest trees is usually 15 to 20 days earlier at St. Paul than at Ely.

The following list of approximate dates of flowering periods may be useful in planning trips to see wildflowers:

Skunk Cabbage (Twin Cities)	April 10–May 10
Early woodland wildflowers (southeast)	April 10–May 1
Early woodland wildflowers (Twin Cities)	April 15–May 15
Early prairie wildflowers, especially Pasque Flower (south and southwest)	April 15–May 15
Late prairie wildflowers (central sandplain)	June 1–July 1
Prickly Pear (southwest)	July 1–15
Summer roadside wildflowers (central and north)	July 15–30
Muskeg and bog wildflowers (north)	June 20–July 15
North Shore wildflowers, especially Flowering Raspberry and Tall Lungwort	July 1–15
Summer prairie wildflowers (south and east)	July 15–August 15
Floodplain wildflowers along St. Croix River	August 1–30
Lotus Lilies at Lake Minnetonka (if still present, upper lake)	August 10–20
Summer wildflowers (Twin Cities)	July 15–August 15
Autumn wildflowers (southern and western prairies)	August 1–frost
Autumn wildflowers (northern forest)	August 1–frost
Wild Rice harvest (northern counties)	August 25–September 5

Native Americans and Wild Plants

The Native Americans of the forests and prairies that are now Minnesota and adjacent areas had names and uses for many of the plants considered here as wildflowers. From these and other plants, they obtained food, fiber, construction material, medicines, and items having artistic, magical, and religious uses. Some of these values and uses are referred to elsewhere in this book, and sources of additional information may be found in the bibliography.

The Ojibwe of Lake Superior marked the progress of the year by "moons," six of which were named for changes in the vegetation:

Flower Moon	May
Strawberry Moon	June
Raspberry Moon	July
Blueberry Moon	August
Wild Rice Moon	September
Falling Leaf Moon	October

The Ojibwe knew plants, and in their language grouped those that were similar in general appearance or use. According to Edwin James, an early physician and traveler interested in plants, Native Americans, and Native American languages, the Ojibwe classification of the green world was generally as follows:

A.	Meti-goag	Woody plants
B.	Shingobeek	Evergreens
BB.	Ne-bi-shun	Broad-leaved trees and shrubs
AA.	Weah-gush-kean	Herbaceous (nonwoody) plants
B.	Me-zhus-keen	Grasslike plants
BB.	Other kinds	

Plants with edible berries or fruits were also grouped, the Ojibwe names for these often including *min* or *meen*, meaning "berry." Some examples are *manomin* (wild rice, literally "good berry"), *o-da-na-me-na* (strawberry, literally "heart berry"), and *menagha* or *meen* (blue berry).

Berries were eaten in season or dried for winter use on rocks or on frames covered with grass or rush mats. Dried berries were often added to dried meat and fat to make pemmican, used in traveling or as a condensed winter food. The pulp of wild plums was dried after being boiled with maple sugar to form a "leathery substance," which in winter was stewed with dried meat.

Plants producing starchy foods were especially valued. Of these wild rice was the most important. Many Native American villages were located on wild rice stands, and battles were fought between the Dakota (Sioux) and Ojibwe for control of such sites. Harvesting and processing this native grain involved several complicated steps and was a triumph of primitive technology. The grain was gathered, dried, parched, threshed, and winnowed before it was stored indefinitely for food.

On the prairies the principal starchy food was the Prairie Turnip (*Pediomelum esculentum*). This legume, which has a thick root somewhat like a small turnip, was dug and cooked like a common potato; the central starchy part was then eaten. Lycurgus Moyer, a pioneer judge at Montevideo and an excellent botanist, noted that campsites of traveling bands of Dakota were often marked by piles of discarded roots. This plant is now scarce and found only on unplowed prairie remnants.

Arrowhead (*Sagittaria*) tubers were removed from the soft bottoms of shallow lakes and streams by treading the mud with bare feet; the tubers then floated to the surface. They are starchy and much like a small potato, but less firm. The Ojibwe strung and dried these "swan potatoes" and added them to winter stews. Groundnut (*Apios*), a legume with underground chains of tubers ranging from marble-size to 3 inches in diameter, was used by the Menominee in Wisconsin. The tubers were peeled, parboiled, sliced, and dried for winter use. Groundnut was early imported into Europe as a possible crop plant, but cultivation proved impractical because the tubers take several years to develop. The fleshy roots of Yellow Water Lily and American Lotus Lily were also sometimes eaten by Native Americans.

Another American plant that was sent to Europe as a possible food is the Jerusalem Artichoke. This wide-leaved perennial sunflower is quite common on open prairies and sometimes along roads. Its edible tubers, which look much like small knobby potatoes, were used by Native Americans, who sometimes cultivated the plant. Jerusalem Artichoke was imported into Europe around 1600, about the same time as the common potato. It never gained much favor, even though the French explorer Samuel de Champlain thought the tubers tasted like artichoke. *Jerusalem* is the result of linguistic confusion. *Girasol*, literally "turning to the sun," was the name given it in Spain. When imported into England, *girasol* became *Jerusalem*. The tuber is still sold in some stores, often as "sunchoke."

Several wild plants were used for flavoring in Native American cooking. Examples are wild onions and Wild Ginger. According to Frances Densmore, who early in this century gathered much information on plants valued by the Ojibwe, tea was often brewed by the Ojibwe to avoid drinking raw water when traveling. Tea was made from the leaves of plants, including Labrador Tea, Wintergreen, and Red Raspberry. The flowers of various wild plants were also collected throughout the summer, dried, and used later for tea sweetened with maple sugar.

Many of the plants considered here as wildflowers were highly regarded by the Native Americans for their medicinal properties. For the most part such plants have herbage or roots with a strong odor, disagreeable taste, milky or colored juice, and drastic, even poisonous, properties. Many were also used by white settlers and early physicians, and a few are still used. Frances Densmore lists 69 medicinal plants used by both Native Americans and Whites. Among them are Yarrow, Sweet Flag, Wintergreen, Labrador Tea, Cup Plant, Culver's Root, Boneset, Blue Cohosh, Baneberry, Bloodroot, and Milkweed.

Often the roots were collected, dried, and stored in special medicine bags. Knowledge of medicinal plants was part of the Native American culture and was based largely on generations of practical experience. However, the medicinal or magical properties were sometimes revealed in dreams. Among the Ojibwe, information on identification and application of medicinal plants was passed down to initiates and members of the Midewiwin Lodge, to which many males belonged. Often the medicine men who dispensed medicinal herbs specialized in only a few kinds. Information on other herbs was sometimes purchased by one medicine man from another. Like the present-day physician, the Native American medicine man charged patients for specialized knowledge and services rendered.

Medicine in Native American culture was not sharply separated from magic or even music. Roots were thought to be especially potent both because they obtained strength from the earth and because they were dug by the bear, an animal they especially revered.

Indian Hemp and its close relative Dogbane have a thin but tough fibrous bark. This was "spun" into cordage, twine, and thread by rolling it against the thigh with the palm of the hand and was used for bowstrings and fishnets. Mats were made from leaves of cattails and stems of bulrushes, first softened by boiling, then dried, and woven or plaited when dampened and pliable. Cattail down was used as disposable diaper material, packed around the infant on the cradle board and often mixed with dry sphagnum moss and punky wood. The down was also stuffed inside moccasins for winter warmth.

Wildflower Immigrants

Many of our roadside wildflowers of summer are naturalized Americans. They came as immigrants, mostly from Europe, some from gardens and dooryards, some as crop and drug plants, and some, uninvited and unwanted, as weeds to follow and plague the farmer. Common examples are Common Sow Thistle, Creeping Jenny, Field Thistle, Leafy Spurge, and Dandelion.

Following is a sampling by color of the more respected plant immigrants brought from foreign gardens and dooryards to new homes here. These plants later escaped to roadsides, fields, and waste corners, where they can still be found. They may be used to re-create flower and herb gardens of the 1800s, with some vigorous hoeing now and then to keep them in their place. However, if allowed to escape, they may become weedy, seriously displacing native plants.

Yellow	Butter-and-eggs, Moneywort, Tansy, Yellow Flag, Cypress Spurge
Blue and purple	European Bellflower, Ground Ivy, Chicory, Sweet Rocket, Catnip
White	Common Yarrow, Ox-eye Daisy, Common Valerian

| Pink | Bouncing Bet |
| Orange | Tawny Day Lily |

The trailing and low-growing plants, such as Ground Ivy, Moneywort, and Cypress Spurge, were often planted on graves and can still be found in old cemeteries.

Eating Wildflowers—Don't!

Wildflowers are to be seen and, along with other wild plants, are usually not to be eaten. The safe approach is not to eat any wild plant or any part of it unless you are certain of its identification and edibility. The idea that wild plants provide a natural smorgasbord of delicacies that can be gathered and eaten with impunity is both fallacious and dangerous. Many wild plants are poisonous. Native Americans and country people have long been aware of this.

Part of the long history of plants is their development of means to avoid being eaten by insects and other herbivores. Plants have many obvious survival stratagems such as thorns, spines, harsh leaves, and woodiness. Plants also produce and store a wide variety of protective organic chemicals. These range in properties from objectionable taste to very poisonous. Toxicity often depends on the kind of animal that eats the plant and is sometimes quite specific. Any plant readily available and palatable to all kinds of herbivores would likely not long survive.

Plants that are poisonous or have other drastic or unpleasant effects on humans and their domestic animals are widely distributed in the plant kingdom. They are especially common in the crowfoot, parsley, lobelia, milkweed, dogbane, barberry, poppy, nightshade, arum, iris, and lily families. The unpalatability of others, such as Locoweed in the bean family and Common Wormwood and Western Ironweed in the composite family, ensures that they will thrive in overgrazed pastures. One of the most interesting cases of differential toxicity is Common St. John's-wort, which is toxic to light-colored but not to dark-colored grazing animals.

Often objectionable substances are more concentrated in the roots than in other plant parts. Although roots have long been used as a source of medicinal drugs, eating roots of wild plants is especially chancy. People have died from eating a small piece of Water Hemlock root, possibly mistaking it for wild carrot.

For more information on this subject, see the books by Muenscher, Foster, and Duke, and Fernald, Kinsey, and Rollins listed in the bibliography.

Wildflowers in the Garden

This book is not a treatise on horticulture, but since many wildflowers are available from nurseries and seed companies, a few comments on wildflower culture may be useful.

In general, wildflowers that are natives of other areas, especially of Eurasia, and have become naturalized along roads and in other places present few cultural difficulties. Often they were originally garden plants or came as colorful stowaways and, as previously indicated, thrive with little care. We refer to plants like Bouncing Bet, Tawny Day Lily, Butter-and-eggs, Sweet Rocket, Ground Ivy, Ox-eye Daisy, Tansy, and European Bellflower. The principal difficulty is keeping them under control. They tend to be weedy but, in their own fashion, are quite ornamental. Even Creeping Jenny, which has had bad press and is more politely called Field Bindweed, makes an attractive plant in an outdoor hanging basket.

Raising native wildflowers, however, is more difficult. Many are fussy about soil chemistry, especially alkalinity or acidity (pH), and have quite specific requirements for soil moisture and shade. Since each has different needs, the only general rule is the rule of thumb that they grow best under conditions similar to those in which they are found in the wild. Bog plants thrive in bogs, prairie plants in prairie conditions, and woodland flowers in shady places.

Some of the most successful native plants in our shady dooryard at Minnetonka, where the soil is quite limy, have been Wild Blue Phlox, Canada Violet, and Star-flowered False Solomon's Seal. Harebell is easily grown in the rockery. Virginia Blue-bell does well with daffodils in moister spots. We have been unsuccessful with plants that thrive in acid sandy areas, such as Carolina Puccoon, Butterflyweed, and Pansy Violet. By contrast, Bracted Spiderwort, which often grows on acid sandy soil, does well and is very showy.

Lady's-slippers, now available from some nurseries, require special care and stable situations where they can remain undisturbed for many years. The Stemless Lady's-slipper requires acid soil, but the Showy and Yellow Lady's-slippers require soil that is neutral to somewhat alkaline. Field mice can be troublesome in winter because they eat the underground parts. In general, raising lady's-slippers is too uncertain for most amateur gardeners, and we conclude it is better to enjoy these plants in the wild. False Dragonhead (*Physostegia*) and Cardinal Flower are showy wildflowers that can be bought from nurseries. The former does well in the perennial garden if given plenty of water, and the latter practically requires wet feet. New England Aster is easily grown and makes a robust, colorful garden plant that flowers from late summer until frost.

Transplanting spring woodland wildflowers is usually futile, especially when the flowers are in bloom. Even as they bloom, these plants are storing food and forming new underground parts. The stored food is necessary for growth the next spring. If you transplant a Trillium in bloom, you will probably kill it. The same is true of lilies and many other wild plants. To grow wildflowers in the garden, it is prudent to use seed or stock collected or grown locally as it is likely to be adapted to local conditions. Some wildflowers, such as Pasque Flower and Virginia Bluebell, are easily raised from seed.

A useful book on growing native wildflowers is *The Wildflower Book, East of the Rockies: An Easy Guide to Growing and Identifying Wildflowers* by Donald and Lillian

Stokes. An older book, still useful, is *Pioneering with Wildflowers* by George D. Aiken, retired U.S. senator from Vermont, where for many years he operated a wildflower nursery. Catalogs of wildflower nurseries also supply much helpful cultural advice.

Conservation of Wildflowers

Early explorers and settlers often viewed wildflowers as part of a landscape destined to be reshaped by plow and axe; wheat and corn lands were needed, and logs and lumber for building. There were exceptions. Some plants were used as medicinal herbs and spring greens. Children gathered spring flowers for May baskets, and one prairie farm wife, probably reflecting the sentiments of many, noted in a diary that she admired the prairie wildflowers but "supposed it was sinful." Some early explorers, especially S. H. Long and J. N. Nicollet, collected plant specimens and sent them east to such botanical savants as Asa Gray and John Torrey. Others published lists and catalogs of native plants they had found.

The first attempt at a complete catalog of Minnesota higher plants was made by Warren Upham, who published a list of 1,650 kinds (species and varieties) in 1883. Of these, 1,582 were flowering plants. This list was published by the Minnesota Geological and Natural History Survey and included records of earlier botanists, some of them schoolteachers. Upham first mapped the boundary between the wooded region and the prairie in Minnesota, while driving along the edge with a horse and buggy.

Official interest in Minnesota flora—except, of course, for the pines that fed the sawmills—developed near the end of the nineteenth century. In 1889, 1890, and 1891 the legislature sponsored, as part of the Geological and Natural History Survey of Minnesota, a botanical survey of the state. The work was done under the direction of Conway MacMillan, then professor of botany at the University of Minnesota. The resulting report is a thick, technical volume titled *The Metaspermae of the Minnesota Valley.* In it can be found all that was known about Minnesota plants up to that time, including a list of earlier publications. MacMillan also wrote a less technical book, titled *Minnesota Plant Life,* published in 1899.

The Showy, or Pink-and-White, Lady's-slipper achieved its status as the official Minnesota state flower, or "floral emblem," only after botanical and legal difficulties. The confusion occurred because six different species of lady's-slipper orchids grow in Minnesota. In 1892 plans were made for a Minnesota exhibit for the World's Fair at Chicago—the famous Columbian Exposition. Before that time, Minnesota had no official flower. Accounts of what happened differ, but apparently the Women's Auxiliary of the Board of Fair Managers urged the legislature to adopt as a floral emblem the Wild Lady's-slipper, or Moccasin Flower, *Cypripedium calceolus.* The legislature did that, and the 1893 *Legislative Manual* has a rather poor illustration, probably of the Showy Lady's-slipper, with a caption noting that six kinds of lady's-slippers grow in Minnesota. But errors and uncertainties had crept in. First, the true Moccasin

Flower, although a lady's-slipper, has leafless stems and rosy flowers and is not the more robust Showy. Second, the botanical name recommended is that of the European Yellow Lady's-slipper. Minnesota's two yellow kinds, the Small Yellow and the Large Yellow Lady's-slipper, are often considered to be varieties of this species. To confuse matters further, the lady's-slipper on the state flag was white, and many of the early Blue Books picture a bouquet of lady's-slippers of assorted colors.

Nearly ten years of lady's-slipper confusion went by, and then in 1902 the ladies of the St. Anthony Study Circle straightened it out and, through Mrs. E. C. Chatfield of Minneapolis, persuaded the legislature to modify the statutes so that there was no doubt about the identity of the Minnesota state flower. It was designated and has remained the Showy Lady's-slipper.

The first public wildflower garden in Minnesota, now called the Eloise Butler Wildflower and Bird Sanctuary, was established in Glenwood Park, Minneapolis, in 1907. In an account of its establishment in the Proceedings of the Minnesota Academy of Science for 1910, Miss Butler noted that "teachers of botany and other interested citizens petitioned the Park Board to set aside a tract of land for a wild, botanic garden." It was opened to the public on April 20, 1907, a historic date for wildflower conservation and appreciation. Miss Butler taught botany in Minneapolis schools and had a special interest in algae as well as in wildflowers.

As the population of Minnesota increased, concern grew for some of the rarer and more colorful wildflowers. Unrestricted picking, especially of flowers for sale, was causing some kinds to become scarce. Therefore, in 1925, the legislature passed a protective law, *The Conservation of Certain Wildflowers* (Minn. Statute 17.23). This law, with amendments made in 1935, prohibits the taking, buying, and selling of lady's-slippers and other orchids, trilliums, lilies, gentians, arbutus, and lotus from public lands without permission of the Minnesota Commissioner of Agriculture, and from private lands without permission of both the landowner and the commissioner. The protected wildflowers "may not be dug, cut, plucked, pulled, or gathered in any manner." Violation is a misdemeanor, and fine or imprisonment is the penalty.

The law was helpful, at least in the Minnetonka area. Yellow Lady's-slippers, which according to older residents, nearly disappeared early in this century, returned to become moderately abundant in hardwood forests. Unfortunately they have again become scarce because of land development.

It should be emphasized that other restrictions on taking wildflowers and other plants from public lands, such as forests, parks, and wildlife areas, are in force. Information can be obtained from the local land manager. For example, in state parks it is illegal to take plants or plant parts of any kind.

In addition to legal protection and preservation, some management of suitable habitats is often essential. Prairie plants, for example, may benefit from occasional burning over of the area or from moderate grazing, both of which simulate original prairie conditions. Water must be retained in bogs and marshes. In forested areas some kinds of wildflowers are favored by cutting of trees and brush, but others are not. Yellow and Showy Lady's-slippers, for instance, are forest plants but thrive best in open forests where they are not shaded out by dense growth of trees and brush.

In Minnesota about one-fourth of the land is in public ownership, but this land is mostly in the northern forested area. Here there is ample space for wildflowers. In the south and west, however, the original prairies are now mostly farmland. Here some parcels of undisturbed lands, especially low-lying wetlands, have been preserved for waterfowl and other wildlife, largely through the efforts of state and federal agencies and financed by sportsmen's money. Since the mid-1960s, the Minnesota Department of Natural Resources Scientific and Natural Areas Program has worked to preserve undisturbed plant communities and rare and endangered species habitat.

Privately financed organizations of natural history enthusiasts and others who are ecologically minded have also done much for wildflowers. The Minnesota Chapter of The Nature Conservancy has acquired and permanently preserved many choice natural areas, including remnants of unbroken upland prairie. This nonprofit organization deserves the support of those interested in wildflowers. Other organizations that have helped and still are helping to preserve our wildflower heritage are the Minnesota Native Plant Society, the Audubon Society, the Minnesota Horticultural Society, the Minnesota Garden Clubs, and the Minnesota Ornithologists' Union. The efforts, interest, and generosity of private and corporate landowners should also be recognized. Some of the better undisturbed natural areas now remain only because someone had the foresight and appreciation to leave them undisturbed as pieces of yesterday's landscape to be enjoyed today and tomorrow—and also was willing to make the effort to preserve them *now*.

White
Flowers

Sharp-lobed Hepatica
(*Hepatica acutiloba*)

Description Perennial woodland wildflower of early spring. The flowers have 5 to 12 (often 6) colored sepals ranging from white through pink, blue, and lavender. They stand on slender, hairy stems on which are 3 green protective bracts. Later a clump of leaves develops. They are often mottled with purple or brown and have 3 pointed lobes. *Early spring*

Habitat and Range Minnesota: upland woods, mostly south and center; general: temperate eastern North America on limy soils.

Sharp-lobed Hepatica

Comments The name refers to the fancied resemblance of the leaf to a liver. The plant was once used to treat liver ailments. Also called Liverleaf.

Related Species The Round-lobed Hepatica (*Hepatica americana*) has similar flowers, but the leaves have blunt or rounded lobes. It prefers acid soil and in Minnesota grows mostly in the north and east.

Wood Anemone (*Anemone quinquefolia*)

Description A common spring wildflower of woods. The slender stem, usually less than 6 inches tall, is topped by a whorl of divided leaves above which is a single flower. The flower usually has 5 white, pink, or purplish sepals. Solitary divided leaves also rise from the elongate rhizome. The plants often grow in patches. *Spring*

Habitat and Range Minnesota: throughout much of the state but more common in the south and east; general: temperate eastern North America.

Wood Anemone

Comments *Anemone* is an ancient name, possibly derived from the Greek word for wind, referring to open, windy places where some kinds of plants grow. Also called Mayflower.

Canada Anemone
(Anemone canadensis)

Canada Anemone

Description Robust perennial, usually 1 to 2 feet tall, of moist, open places. It often grows in patches. The plant has deeply lobed basal leaves and an upright stem bearing a cluster (whorl) of cut leaves from which the long-stalked white flowers rise. They are 1 to 1½ inches across and have 5, sometimes 4, petal-like sepals. *Spring, early summer*

Habitat and Range Minnesota: throughout, often along roads and railways; general: much of temperate North America but not in the Far West.

Long-fruited Thimbleweed

Comments Also called Canada Windflower. Worldwide there are about 85 species of *Anemone*, some of which are raised for the beauty of their flowers. All have a whorl of leaves on the stem, above which the flowers rise.

Long-fruited Thimbleweed
(Anemone cylindrica)

Description Plant of dry, open places. It has clumped basal leaves and an upright stem with a whorl of 3 or more deeply lobed and cut leaves. The long-stalked, dish-shaped flowers are about 1 inch across and have 5 greenish white sepals. Fruits (achenes) are in an elongate cluster, 2 to 5 times longer than wide, that resembles the rough part of a thimble. When mature, the achenes are covered with matted, cottony hairs. *Summer*

Habitat and Range Minnesota: throughout; general: temperate North America.

Related Species The Virginia Thimbleweed (*Anemone virginiana*) is similar but has a shorter "thimble," about twice as long as wide. It is mostly a plant of open woods and clearings.

Rue Anemone
(Thalictrum thalictroides)

Rue Anemone

Description This graceful spring wildflower is quite similar to the true anemones. The slender stems, often clumped, rise from a tuft of compound basal leaves, each with 9 leaflets. Near the top of the stem is a whorl of leaflets and several slender-stalked flowers with 4 to 10 white or rose pink sepals. The fruits, as in *Anemone*, are achenes. Elongate tubers are produced at the base of the upright stems. *Spring*

Habitat and Range Minnesota: rich upland forests and clearings, mostly in the southeastern third; general: eastern United States.

Comments There is a cultivar with double flowers. Double flowers also occur in the wild occasionally.

False Rue Anemone *(Enemion biternatum)*

Description Superficially much like Rue Anemone but different in several respects. The white flowers rise in the axils of scattered stem leaves and not above a whorl of leaflets. The fruit is a pod (follicle) containing seeds, and the roots are fibrous with small tubers along them. *Spring*

Habitat and Range Minnesota: southeastern third; general: eastern United States and adjacent Canada.

Comments A common and beautiful spring wildflower of moist woods and floodplain forests, where it often grows in patches covering the forest floor.

False Rue Anemone

Virgin's Bower
(*Clematis virginiana*)

Description Sprawling or climbing vine with square stems and opposite, compound leaves with 3 leaflets. Leaf stalks twist around other objects. The small flowers are clustered and have 4 creamy white sepals. Later the flowers develop into beardlike tufts of plumed achenes. *Summer*

Habitat and Range Minnesota: throughout in open or semishady places; general: temperate eastern North America.

Comments This ornamental perennial vine is easily grown on a trellis or can be used as a trailing ground cover. Also called Old Man's Beard.

RICHARD HAUG

Virgin's Bower

Related Species The Purple Virgin's Bower (*Clematis verticillaris*) has large blue flowers much like those of a garden clematis. In Minnesota it grows in rocky, wooded, and brushy places, mostly in the east and northeast.

Prairie Larkspur

Prairie Larkspur
(*Delphinium carolinianum* subsp. *virescens*)

Description Perennial of dry prairies and open hillsides. The stems, usually 1 to 3 feet tall, end in a spikelike cluster of white flowers. Each flower has 5 sepals, the uppermost ending in a spur, and 4 crowded irregular petals in the center. Both basal and stem leaves are much cut and divided. *Late spring, summer*

Habitat and Range Minnesota: south and west; general: prairies and plains of central and western North America.

Comments New growth is toxic to cattle. *Delphinium* stems from the Latin word for dolphin and refers to the fancied resemblance of the spurred flower to this aquatic mammal.

Tall Meadow Rue
(Thalictrum dasycarpum)

Description A wind-pollinated member of the Crowfoot Family. It has plumes of small flowers in which the showy parts are the dangling white or yellow stamens (on plants with male flowers) or the purplish clusters of pistils (on plants with female flowers). This clumped perennial of moist meadows and brushy places is often taller than 3 feet. Leaflets of the compound leaves are longer than wide and end in 3 pointed lobes. *Late spring, summer*

Habitat and Range Minnesota: throughout; general: much of temperate North America.

Tall Meadow Rue

Early Meadow Rue
(Thalictrum dioicum)

Description Early Meadow Rue is similar to Tall Meadow Rue but less robust. It commonly grows in moist woods as clumps 1 to 2 feet tall. Leaflets are about as wide as long and end in 3 blunt lobes. *Spring*

Habitat and Range Minnesota: throughout; general: temperate eastern North America.

Related Species The Veiny Meadow Rue (*Thalictrum venulosum*) of prairies and open places with coarse soil is similar but has leaflets with a rough pattern of veins beneath and scattered stems rising from running rootstocks.

Red Baneberry *(Actaea rubra)*

Description Perennial of woods. It is usually 1 to 2 feet tall with a clumped, bushy appearance and

Early Meadow Rue

Red Baneberry (fruit)

has compound leaves with many sharply toothed leaflets. In spring the plant bears a fluffy cluster of small white flowers, and in summer shiny red or, sometimes, white berries. Each berry is on a slender stalk. *Spring*

Habitat and Range Minnesota: throughout; general: temperate North America.

Red Baneberry

Related Species The similar White Baneberry (*Actaea pachypoda*), also called Doll's Eyes, is more robust and has berries that are usually white with a dark spot, "the pupil." The berries stand out from the stem on thick, reddish stalks. In Minnesota White Baneberry is most common in the southeast. Berries and roots of both species are poisonous.

WATER LILY FAMILY
(*Nymphaeaceae*)

White Water Lily (*Nymphaea odorata* subsp. *tuberosa*)

Description Common in shallow water, especially along lakeshores where the bottom is mucky. The floating leaves are circular, deeply notched at the base, and green beneath. The double white flower is about 6 inches across and has petals that merge with the stamens, forming a continuous, transitional series. Short branches of the rootstocks sometimes break off and form new plants. *Summer*

White Water Lilly

Habitat and Range Minnesota: throughout; general: eastern United States and adjacent Canada.

Related Species The similar Sweet-scented White Water Lily (*Nymphaea odorata* subsp. *oderata*) has leaves that are purplish beneath, and sweet-scented flowers sometimes tinged with pink. In Minnesota it is most common in the north.

POPPY FAMILY
(*Papaveraceae*)

Bloodroot
(*Sanguinaria canadensis*)

Description An early spring wildflower of moist rich woods. The elongate buds, which are first protected by 2 green sepals and sheathed in a rolled-up leaf, open as pristine white flowers. They have 8 or 12 petals and a golden tuft of stamens.

Bloodroot

The petals soon drop, and an elongate seed pod develops. Leaves are basal and stalked, and have wide, irregularly lobed blades. *Spring*

Habitat and Range Minnesota: throughout, except in the extreme west and northeast; general: east, temperate North America.

Dutchman's Breeches

Comments All parts of the plant have orange red juice, which was used by Native Americans for war paint and dye.

FUMITORY FAMILY
(*Fumariaceae*)

Dutchman's Breeches
(*Dicentra cucullaria*)

Description Low perennial of rich woods. It has much-divided leaves in a basal clump and slender, often arching stems along which are the nodding white or, sometimes, pink flowers. They have 4 petals, 2 extending backward as blunt, spreading spurs: the "legs" of the "breeches." They contain nectar that can be reached by long-tongued moths and by bees strong enough to push apart the petals. *Spring*

Habitat and Range Minnesota: widely distributed, but most common in the southeast; general: temperate eastern North America.

Comments The small, clustered tubers contain alkaloids and were once used medicinally. Cows have been poisoned by eating them.

BARBERRY FAMILY (*Berberidaceae*)

May Apple (*Podophyllum peltatum*)

Description A deciduous forest perennial, 1 to 2 feet tall, characterized by shiny umbrella-like leaves, often up to 1 foot across. The short upright stem is topped with 1 to 3 (usually 2) deeply lobed leaves. The large nodding waxy white flower is hidden in the fork between them. Single-leaved plants do not bloom. The plant spreads by running rootstocks and may form large patches. The ripe fruit resembles a small, pale lemon. *Spring*

May Apple

Habitat and Range Minnesota: southeastern Minnesota; general: Quebec to Florida and Texas.

Comments It is sometimes eaten, but the seeds are poisonous, as are the leaves, stems, and underground parts. The plant, especially the roots, contains toxic resins and was used as a purgative, but people sometimes died. It has been investigated for use against skin cancer but has caused severe side effects. Cattle avoid eating it.

MUSTARD FAMILY (*Cruciferae*)

Toothwort (*Cardamine concatenata*)

Description A spring wildflower that often grows in patches in moist woods. The stem, usually less than a foot tall, ends in a cluster of 4-petaled white or pink flowers, each about ½ inch across. They stand above a whorl of stem leaves that are deeply lobed and coarsely toothed. *Spring*

Habitat and Range Minnesota: mostly in the southeastern third but occasionally northward to St. Louis County; general: temperate eastern North America.

Comments The common name refers to segments of the rootstock that somewhat resemble teeth.

Toothwort

Spring Cress

Spring Cress
(Cardamine bulbosa)

Description A low perennial, usually less than a foot tall, of marshes, wet meadows, and spring areas. The 4-petaled white flowers are in a fairly compact cluster, and the stems are smooth and leafy. Blades of lower leaves are rounded. Small tubers develop at the base of the stem. *Spring*

Habitat and Range Minnesota: throughout, except in the northeast; general: much of temperate eastern North America.

Related Species Other common white-flowered mustards include Water Cress (*Nasturtium officinale*), the brittle-stemmed salad plant of limy streams and springy areas, and Hoary Alyssum (*Berteroa incana*), a weedy annual of dry, open places. The latter has 4 notched white petals and is gray with stiff hairs. Seed pods are globular.

SAXIFRAGE FAMILY
(*Saxifragaceae*)

Bishop's Cap (*Mitella diphylla*)

Description A low, graceful perennial of moist woods. It has basal leaves with heart-shaped blades that are lobed and toothed. The slender stem bears a pair of small leaves and ends in an elongate inflorescence of small white flowers. Each flower has 5 sepals and 5 fringed petals. Flowers resemble miniature snowflakes. *Spring, summer*

Habitat and Range Minnesota: mostly in the southeast and south; general: temperate eastern North America.

Comments Also called Mitrewort.

Bishop's Cap

RICHARD HAUG

Northern Bishop's Cap
(*Mitella nuda*)

Description Northern species has flowers similar to those of the Bishop's Cap, but they are on a leafless stem. Leaves are all basal with rounded, shallowly lobed blades. The upper leaf surface has short, upright hairs. *Late spring, early summer*

Habitat and Range Minnesota: a wide-ranging species of northern wet woods and bogs; general: northeastern United States and Canada.

Comments The name refers to the shape of the pod.

Northern Grass of Parnassus
(*Parnassia palustris*)

Description Low plant of shores and marshes. Characterized by a

Northern Bishop's Cap

basal clump of rounded somewhat heart-shaped leaves. The slender stem bears a single small leaf and ends in a solitary white flower that has 5 spreading petals. *Summer*

Habitat and Range Minnesota: mostly in the center and north; general: circumpolar; in North America from the Arctic south to northern United States.

Related Species The similar Thick-leaved Grass of Parnassus (*Parnassia glauca*) has bluish green leaf blades that are rounded or somewhat tapering at the base. In Minnesota it is found mostly in wet places along the prairie edges from the southeast to northwest.

EVELYN MOYLE

Northern Grass of Parnassus

ROSE FAMILY (*Rosaceae*)

Tall Cinquefoil

Tall Cinquefoil (*Potentilla arguta*)

Description Erect perennial, 1 to 3 feet tall, of dry prairies, fields, and open woods. Stems are usually clumped and have pinnately compound leaves covered with soft, white hairs. Flowers are pale yellow to almost white. *Summer*

Habitat and Range Minnesota: throughout; general: subarctic North America south to central United States.

Related Species The Sulfur Cinquefoil (*Potentilla recta*) is also an upright plant of dry fields and prairies. It has spreading clusters of deep yellow flowers, about 1 inch across. Leaves are palmately compound with 5 to 7 coarsely toothed leaflets. This European plant is widely naturalized in the eastern United States.

Three-toothed Cinquefoil
(Potentilla tridentata)

Description Low plant, usually less than 6 inches tall, with a woody base. It has compound leaves with 3 thick leaflets, each ending in 3 coarse teeth. Its small white flowers are in a spreading cluster. *Summer*

Three-toothed Cinquefoil

Habitat and Range Minnesota: dry, open places, often on sand or rocks. Common on cliffs along Lake Superior; general: sub-arctic North America south to eastern United States.

Comments This cinquefoil is sometimes planted as an interesting and hardy ground cover.

Flowering Raspberry *(Rubus parviflorus)*

Description One of the most conspicuous early summer wildflowers along roads near Lake Superior. The unarmed, woody, and herbaceous stems are commonly 2 to 4 feet tall and have wide, lobed leaves, somewhat like maple leaves. The showy white flowers, about 2 inches across, have 5 spreading petals and many stamens. The stamens are pale when the flower first appears, but they darken with age. *Summer*

Habitat and Range Minnesota: mostly in the northeast; general: from Ontario westward to northwestern North America. It is abundant on Isle Royale in Lake Superior.

Comments The flat, orange red raspberries have a rather bland flavor but make tasty jam. Also called Thimbleberry.

Flowering Raspberry

White Clover

Bean Family
(*Fabaceae*)

White Clover
(*Trifolium repens*)

Description Low perennial of open, grassy places. The creeping stems and rootstocks bear compound leaves, each with 3 finely toothed leaflets, and rounded heads of small white flowers. Each head is on a slender, leafless stalk. *Late spring, summer*

Habitat and Range A European species that has long been planted as a component of pastures and lawns, and is widely naturalized on well-drained soils.

Comments It is probably the true Irish shamrock.

Related Species Alsike Clover (*Trifolium hybridum*) is similar but has pink, markedly sweet-scented flowers on upright, leafy stems. It is also of European origin, coming from Alsike, Sweden. Frequently it has escaped from hayfields to roadsides.

Canada Milk-vetch (*Astragalus canadensis*)

Description Robust, often clumped perennial with erect stems 1 to 4 feet tall. It has pinnately compound leaves with many leaflets, and elongate, rather loose clusters of white or yellowish flowers. These are followed by short, ascending pods. *Summer*

Habitat and Range Minnesota: throughout on moist prairies, along streams, and in open woods; general: much of temperate United States and adjacent Canada.

Canada Milk-vetch

Seneca Snakeroot

MILKWORT FAMILY
(*Polygalaceae*)

Seneca Snakeroot
(*Polygala senega*)

Description Perennial of dry prairies and open woods. The slender, unbranched, and usually clumped stems rise from a thick taproot. Generally they are 6 to 12 inches tall and end in a tapering cluster of small white flowers. *Summer*

Habitat and Range Minnesota: throughout, except in the northeast and southwest; general: temperate eastern North America.

Comments The roots contain bitter substances and oil of wintergreen, which once had medicinal uses. Seneca Indians valued them for treating snakebite. The Potawatomi called this plant "Indian Head Dress," likening the flower-tipped stems to feathers of a subterranean warrior.

Flowering Spurge

SPURGE FAMILY
(*Euphorbiaceae*)

Flowering Spurge
(*Euphorbia corollata*)

Description Erect, often clumped perennial, usually 1 to 2 feet tall, with spreading clusters of white "flowers," each with 5 "petals." The apparent flower is really a much reduced inflorescence. The leaves have no teeth and are alternate, except for a whorl below the inflorescence. Juice is milky. *Summer*

Habitat and Range Minnesota: old fields, open woods, roadsides, and prairies, mostly in the southeast; general: eastern United States.

Sweet White Violet
(*Viola macloskeyi*
subsp. *pallens*)

Description Low,
tufted perennial of
bogs, marshes, and
shores. The small
white flowers are
sweet-scented and
marked with purple
along the veins.
Leaves are heart-
shaped, all basal, and
hairless. The plants
spread by slender run-
ners to form patches.
Spring, summer

RICHARD HAUG

Sweet White Violet

Habitat and Range
Minnesota: mostly in
the north and east; general: subarctic and temperate North America.

Related Species Several other species have sweet-scented white flowers. Kidney-leaved
White Violet (*Viola renifolia*) has hairy, kidney-shaped leaves; Lance-leaved Violet
(*Viola lanceolata*), narrow elongate leaves; and Swamp White Violet (*Viola incognita*),
heart-shaped leaves that are hairy
on one or both sides. All have only
basal leaves and grow in moist
places.

Canada Violet (*Viola canadensis*)

Description Woodland violet with
conspicuous white flowers, often
tinged with pink or purple, and
having yellowish centers. There
are both basal and stem leaves
with wide heart-shaped blades.
Var. *rugulosa* has runners and rootstocks, whereby it spreads to form
patches. *Spring, summer*

Habitat and Range Minnesota:
widespread but most common
in the south; general: temperate
North America.

Canada Violet

40

EVENING PRIMROSE FAMILY
(*Onagraceae*)

Nuttall's Evening Primrose
(*Oenothera nuttallii*)

Description The largest flowered Minnesota Evening Primrose. The white or pinkish flowers are nearly 2 inches across. It grows up to 2 feet tall and has whitish stem fibers and nodding flower buds. *Summer*

Habitat and Range Minnesota: prairies, mostly in the northwest; general: temperate western North America.

EVELYN MOYLE

Nuttall's Evening Primrose

RICHARD HAUG

Enchanter's Nightshade

Enchanter's Nightshade
(*Circaea quadrisulcata*)

Description Woodland perennial, usually 1 to 2 feet tall, with opposite, oval leaves and slender clusters of small white flowers. Flower parts are in twos. The small, pear-shaped fruits are bristly with hooked hairs that cling to clothing. *Summer*

Habitat and Range Minnesota: common in woods; general: widespread in eastern North America. Also in Asia.

Comments The enchanter referred to in the name is the "clinging" enchantress Circe, who detained Ulysses on his travels.

Related Species Smaller Enchanter's Nightshade (*Circaea alpina*) is similar but is 3 to 8 inches tall and grows in wet woods and swamps, mostly in the north.

Wild Sarsaparilla

Aralia Family
(Araliaceae)

Wild Sarsaparilla
(Aralia nudicaulis)

Description Common perennial of forests. The leafy plants, about 1 foot tall, are really spreading, 3-part compound leaves, each on an upright stalk. They rise from rootstocks that also bear leafless stems ending in 3 clusters (umbels) of greenish white flowers. In late summer these develop into purplish black berries. *Summer*

Habitat and Range Minnesota: throughout in wooded areas but most common in the north; general: temperate North America.

Comments The berries are eaten by bears and foxes, and the aromatic rootstocks were once used in folk medicine and for flavoring root beer.

American Spikenard
(Aralia racemosa)

Description Stout perennial of rich woods. Stems are often 3 to 6 feet long and somewhat arching. It has large, spreading compound leaves with many leaflets. The small white flowers are in an elongate, much-branched inflorescence. They are followed by small purple berries. *Summer*

American Spikenard

American Spikenard (fruit)

42

Habitat and Range Minnesota: throughout in woods; general: temperate eastern North America.

Comments The stout root is aromatic and once had medicinal uses. It was also used to flavor root beer. The berries have been used for jelly.

CARROT FAMILY (*Apiaceae*)

Wild Carrot (*Daucus carota*)

Description The ancestor of the garden carrot. This European biennial grows on roadsides, in old fields, and in waste places. The stem, usually 1 to 2 feet tall, bears elongate, much divided leaves and conspicuous, flat clusters (compound umbels) of small white flowers. The center flower of the umbel is often purple. The umbels face the sky during the day but bend downward at night. When in fruit, the branches of the umbel curve upward in a bird's-nest pattern. *Summer*

Habitat and Range Widely distributed as a weedy plant throughout Minnesota and elsewhere in North America.

Comments Also called Queen Anne's Lace.

Water Hemlock (*Cicuta maculata*)

Description It is usually 3 to 6 feet tall and has large compound leaves with toothed leaflets. The small white flowers are grouped in compound clusters (umbels) that are several inches across. *Summer*

Habitat and Range Minnesota: throughout; general: subarctic and temperate North America.

EVELYN MOYLE

Wild Carrot

Water Hemlock

Comments Also called Musquash Root and Spotted Cowbane. Our most poisonous plant. It contains a poisonous resin, cicutatoxin, concentrated in the elongate tubers at the base of the stem. Ingestion of a small piece of tuber is sufficient to cause convulsions and death in humans. Water Hemlock grows in marshes, roadside ditches, and along streams. Cattle can eat the leaves and stems, fresh or as hay, apparently without harm, but they have been killed by pulling up the plants and eating the roots.

Water Parsnip (*Sium suave*)

Description Perennial, usually 2 to 4 feet tall, of wet marshes, quiet waters, and shores. It is remarkable for variation in the shape of the leaves. Aerial leaves are pinnately compound with quite ordinary, elongate, toothed leaflets, but submerged leaves are much cut and divided. The small white flowers are in spreading compound umbels. *Summer*

Water Parsnip

Habitat and Range Minnesota: throughout, often abundant in forest ponds; general: subarctic North America south through much of United States.

Comments Water Parsnip has sometimes poisoned cattle.

Cow Parsnip (*Heracleum lanatum*)

Description Giant herb, often growing to a height of 8 feet or more. It has large compound leaves with 3 main divisions. Leaflets are hairy beneath, coarsely toothed, and often lobed and heart-shaped at the base. The white flowers are in large, flat clusters (compound umbels). Individual flowers at the edge of the umbel have longer outer than inner petals. *Summer*

Habitat and Range Minnesota: throughout on rich, moist soils, especially along forest edges and roads; general: subarctic and much of temperate North America. Also in Siberia.

Comments *Heracleum* refers to Herakles, the mighty and muscular doer of Greek odd jobs. The Menominee used this plant as a charm to ensure success in deer hunting.

Cow Parsnip

DOGWOOD FAMILY (*Cornaceae*)

Bunchberry
(*Cornus canadensis*)

Description A common, low plant of northern woods and bogs, often in sandy or rocky places. Near the top of the upright stem, usually 3 to 6 inches tall, is a whorl of 4 to 6 spreading elliptical leaves. Above

left, **Bunchberry**
above, **Bunchberry (fruit)**

these is a stalked cluster of small flowers, surrounded by 4 white bracts that resemble petals. In late summer the inflorescence becomes a "bunch" of bright red berries. The plant has elongate underground stems by which it spreads and forms patches. *Spring, summer*

Habitat and Range Minnesota: in the north and east; general: subarctic North America south to northern United States. Also in eastern Asia.

SANDALWOOD FAMILY (*Santalaceae*)

Bastard Toadflax

Bastard Toadflax
(*Comandra umbellata*)

Description Low perennial of prairies, meadows, and open woods. The erect, leafy stems, usually 6 to 12 inches tall, end in a cluster of small white flowers. The stems rise from spreading rootstocks and usually grow in patches. Leaves are oblong to elliptical. *Spring, summer*

Habitat and Range Minnesota: throughout, usually in meadows; general: temperate North America.

Related Species Bastard Toadflax is a semiparasite, its roots attached to those of other plants. The similar Northern Bastard Toadflax (*Geocaulon livida*) is found in northern Minnesota and on Isle Royale. It has juicy, orange red fruits.

Dock-leaved Smartweed

BUCKWHEAT FAMILY (*Polygonaceae*)

Dock-leaved Smartweed
(*Polygonum lapathifolium*)

Description Erect annual, often 3 to 4 feet tall, with long, nodding clusters of small white to rose flowers. The elongate leaves taper to both ends, and the stem is swollen at the nodes and often branched. *Summer*

Habitat and Range Minnesota: widely distributed on damp soils subject to flooding, and as a weed on moist, cultivated soils; general: northern United States and adjacent Canada. Also in Eurasia.

Related Species There are several similar annual smartweeds. The Pennsylvania Smartweed (*Polygonum pensylvanicum*) has blunt, upright clusters of pink or white flowers. It often grows in old fields where the soil is sandy.

Fringed Bindweed (*Polygonum cilinode*)

Description Perennial of open woods, thickets, or rocky places. It has twining, trailing, or sprawling stems that are usually reddish and hairy. Leaves are heart-shaped or arrowhead-shaped, and the numerous white flowers are in loose, fringelike clusters. *Summer*

Habitat and Range Minnesota: mostly in the north and especially common in the northeast; general: temperate North America.

PINK FAMILY
(*Caryophyllaceae*)

Water Chickweed
(*Stellaria aquatica*)

Description Weak-stemmed, but robust, spreading perennial of damp places, espe-

Fringed Bindweed

cially along streams. Often forms patches a foot or more across. The oval, pointed leaves are opposite on the hairy stems, and the white flowers are on forking, upright branches. Each flower is about ½ inch across and has 5 deeply notched petals. *Summer*

Habitat and Range Minnesota: occasional throughout; general: a native of Europe but widespread in temperate North America.

Water Chickweed

Comments *Stellaria* is Latin for "little star," referring to the flower, and the "chick" in chickweed alludes to the former use of the tiny seeds as food for caged song birds.

Related Species Several other chickweeds have smaller flowers. The Common Chickweed (*Stellaria media*) is a weedy annual of gardens and lawns.

Grove Sandwort
(*Arenaria lateriflora*)

Description Low perennial of woods and brushy places. The slender, erect stem, usually less than 8 inches tall, has opposite leaves and 5-petaled white flowers in an upright, forking cluster. The plants have running root-stocks and sometimes grow in patches. *Spring*

Grove Sandwort

Habitat and Range
Minnesota: throughout, often on sandy soil; general: subarctic circumpolar, south in North America to northern United States.

White Campion (*Silene latifolia*)

Description Common roadside plant with white flowers. Usually 1 to 3 feet tall. It has opposite leaves and loose clusters of flowers, each about ¾ inch across and with 5 notched petals that have a flap-like "claw" at the base. Male and female flowers are on different plants. Female flowers have a rounded, bladderlike calyx, and the male flowers a tubular calyx. In the center of the female flower are 5 elongate styles. *Summer*

Habitat and Range A European annual or biennial widely distributed in Minnesota and elsewhere in North America.

Comments *Campion* is an old name referring to fields where such plants often grow.

White Campion

HEATH FAMILY (*Ericaceae*)

Indian Pipe (*Monotropa uniflora*)

Description A remarkable forest plant, usually 3 to 6 inches tall, with upright stems and nodding, pipe-shaped flowers that look as if they were modeled from white wax. Occasionally they are pink, and they always turn black if picked and dried. When in clumps, all the flowers often face the same way. Indian Pipe lives in partnership with a fungus and may also be parasitic on other plants. The stems rise from a mass of thickened roots. *Summer*

Habitat and Range Minnesota: forests in eastern half, often in dense shade; general: widely distributed in North America. Also in eastern Asia.

Indian Pipe

Common Shinleaf
(Pyrola elliptica)

Description Low plant, less than 8 inches tall, of dry woods. It has a tuft of thin, elliptical leaves and erect clusters of nodding white flowers. These have 5 petals and are fragrant. *Summer*

Habitat and Range Minnesota: mostly in the eastern half, often under hardwood trees; general: much of temperate North America. Also in eastern Asia.

Related Species In Minnesota there are several other pyrolas with erect clusters of white or greenish flowers. The One-flowered Shinleaf (*Moneses uniflora*) is a related low plant with a solitary, nodding white flower. It is common in moist woods and bogs in the north.

Common Shinleaf

Labrador Tea
(Ledum groenlandicum)

Description Common low shrub of open and wooded bogs. Usually 1 to 3 feet tall. Twigs are densely hairy. The elongate, evergreen leaves have rolled margins and are densely hairy beneath. Flowers are white with 5 petals and are arranged in spreading, somewhat rounded clusters. *Summer*

Habitat and Range Minnesota: in the north and center, especially in bogs of the coniferous forest area; general: subarctic North America south to northern United States.

Comments The leaves have been used as a substitute for tea.

Labrador Tea

Leatherleaf

Leatherleaf
(Chamaedaphne calyculata)

Description
Common low shrub, 2 to 4 feet tall, of bogs and muskegs. It often grows with the shrubby members of the Heath Family. The nodding white flowers are in the axils of the upper leaves. They have 5 fused petals and are bell-shaped, with a narrow throat. Leaves are thick and evergreen and are alternately arranged on the much branched stems. *Spring*

Habitat and Range Minnesota: common in bogs, especially in the coniferous forest region of the north; general: arctic to temperate regions in both North America and Eurasia.

Wintergreen
(Gaultheria procumbens)

Description Low plant of open woods, usually in sandy or rocky places. The short, erect, branchlike stems rise from slender, trailing or underground stems. Leaves are toothed, elliptical, evergreen, and shiny. The nodding white flowers are followed by edible red berries that sometimes survive the winter. The entire plant has a strong odor of oil of wintergreen (methyl salicylate). *Summer*

Wintergreen

Habitat and Range Minnesota: mostly in the north and east in coniferous forest regions; general: temperate eastern North America.

Comments Native Americans and early explorers made a tea from the leaves that was considered beneficial for rheumatism. Also called Checkerberry.

Wintergreen (fruit)

Trailing Arbutus
(*Epigaea repens*)

Description Low, trailing perennial with hairy, semiwoody stems and elliptical or oblong leaves, 1 to 3 inches in length. The leaves survive the winter. The small pink or white bell-shaped flowers are in clusters and are known for their beauty and fragrance. *Early spring*

Trailing Arbutus

Habitat and Range
Minnesota: northeast and center; general: from Nova Scotia south to Florida, west to Iowa. Because it requires an acid soil in Minnesota, Trailing Arbutus grows mostly in the northeast on sandy or rocky areas, usually under pines or along the edges of sphagnum bogs.

Comments Trailing arbutus is a protected wildflower in Minnesota as it is uncommon and easily destroyed by picking or trampling. Ants visit the ripe fruits, carrying off the seeds, and so may seem to be its principal distributors. The seeds germinate well in moist sand. It is very difficult to cultivate.

PRIMROSE FAMILY (*Primulaceae*)

Star Flower

Star Flower (*Trientalis borealis*)

Description Low perennial of moist woods and bogs, often growing among mosses. The slender, upright stem is usually less than 8 inches tall and rises from an elongate rootstock. The stem is topped by a whorl of leaves of various sizes and by starry, white flowers on slender stalks. Usually the flowers have 7 petals and 7 stamens. *Summer*

Habitat and Range Minnesota: mostly in the north and center; general: subarctic south to temperate United States.

Comments Plants with flower parts in sevens are very rare. In the Linnaean "Sexual System" of plant classification, Star Flower was one of the few plants in Class Heptandra, that is, flowers with 7 stamens.

Gentian Family (*Gentianaceae*)

Buckbean (*Menyanthes trifoliata*)

Description Low perennial of bogs, swamps, and lake margins, sometimes growing in shallow water. Leaves are shiny, have 3 leaflets, and are usually clumped at the end of a thick rootstock. The 5-petaled white flowers are in an elongate, upright cluster, and the upper surface of the petals is covered with curved hairs. *Summer*

Habitat and Range Minnesota: wooded northern two-thirds; general: subarctic circumpolar, south in North America to northern United States.

Comments The juice is bitter, as it is in many members of the gentian family. Gentian root, especially that of the European *Gentiana lutea*, has long been used medicinally as a tonic and also as one of the components of "bitters" in mixed drinks.

Buckbean

Dogbane Family (*Apocynaceae*)

Sessile-leaved Dogbane (*Apocynum sibiricum*)

Description Robust perennial of the prairies. Often grows 3 to 4 feet tall, with erect stems that are branched toward the top. The elliptical leaves clasp the stem or are on very short stalks, and the small white flowers are erect in rather compact clusters. *Summer*

BILL JOHNSON

Sessile-leaved Dogbane

Habitat and Range
Minnesota: throughout; general: temperate North America.

Comments The dogbanes contain a glucoside and are reported to have been used by Native Americans as a fish poison. Their fibrous stems were used by Native Americans to make cordage and fish nets.

Related Species Indian Hemp (*Apocynum cannabinum*) is similar but has leaves that are on short stalks. It grows primarily in open places in southern and western Minnesota.

MILKWEED FAMILY
(*Asclepiadaceae*)

Whorled Milkweed
(*Asclepias verticillata*)

Description A common, white-flowered perennial of dry prairies, roadsides, and other open places. It often grows in patches on poor or shallow soils. The erect stems, usually 6 to 15 inches tall, bear many slender leaves in whorls of 3 to 6, and umbels of small white or greenish white flowers. *Summer*

Habitat and Range Minnesota: throughout, except in the north-east; general: eastern United States and adjacent Canada.

Comments It is poisonous to sheep.

Poke Milkweed
(*Asclepias exaltata*)

Description A beautiful milkweed of moist woods and wooded edges. The stem, usually 2 to 4 feet tall, has opposite leaves that are thin, elliptical, and tapering at both ends. The white or pinkish flowers are borne on slender stalks and are arranged in spreading, often drooping clusters. *Summer*

Habitat and Range Minnesota: mostly in the southeast; general: eastern United States.

RICHARD HAUG

Whorled Milkweed

EVELYN MOYLE

Poke Milkweed

Hedge Bindweed

Morning-glory Family
(*Convolvulaceae*)

Hedge Bindweed
(*Convolvulus sepium*)

Description Perennial twining vine, growing up to 10 feet long on brushy sites and old fences, and sometimes in grassy or marshy places. The large white or pink flowers are bell-shaped and about 2 inches across. They open in the morning and close in the afternoon. Leaves are arrowhead-shaped and alternate on the stem. *Summer*

Habitat and Range Minnesota: throughout; general: widely distributed in eastern and central North America.

Related Species Creeping Jenny (*Convolvulus arvensis*), also called Field Bindweed, is similar but with smaller flowers. It has creeping or low-climbing stems and hairy leaves. The flowers have a waxy, almond odor. This native of Europe is a weedy perennial of open places.

Upright Bindweed (*Convolvulus spithameus*)

Description Slender, erect or feebly twining perennial of open woods and fields, often on sandy soil. The plant is usually less than a foot tall and has hairy alternate leaves. The bell-shaped white flowers are about 1½ inches wide when fully open. *Summer*

Habitat and Range Minnesota: east and north, mostly in coniferous forests; general: temperate eastern North America.

RICHARD HAUG

Upright Bindweed

Dodder (*Cuscuta* spp.)

Description Parasitic plants without green leaves and with slender, yellow or reddish stems that twine around upright stems of other green plants. The small flowers, in compact clusters, are followed by rounded seed pods. Dodder begins growth in late spring from a seed in the soil. However, the vine soon attaches itself to stems of other plants by rootlike structures (haustoria) through which it taps the food-conducting tissue of its host. In moist, lowland forests Dodder often spreads over large patches of herbs. *Summer, autumn*

Habitat and Range Several species occur in Minnesota and are widespread in North America.

Dodder

RICHARD HAUG

MINT FAMILY (*Lamiaceae*)

Wild Mint (*Mentha arvensis*)

Description Common perennial of wet places. The opposite, toothed leaves have a strong minty odor. Flowers are clustered in the axils of normalized stem leaves. They are small and white, pale pink, or pale blue. Stems are often reclining at the base, and the plant is commonly 1 to 2 feet tall. *Summer*

Habitat and Range Minnesota: throughout; general: widely distributed in North America and in Eurasia.

Comments Also called Field Mint and Canada Mint.

Related Species Spearmint (*Mentha spicata*), which sometimes escapes from gardens, has clusters of flowers in the axils of the reduced upper leaves.

Wild Mint

EVELYN MOYLE

55

Catnip (*Nepeta cataria*)

Description Common perennial, naturalized from Eurasia. One to 3 feet tall, with a short spike of white or pale lilac flowers dotted with purple. The lower lip is slightly scalloped. The stalked opposite leaves are soft and arrowhead shaped with coarsely toothed edges. The stems are square and covered with short grayish white hairs. *Summer, early autumn*

Habitat and Range Minnesota: throughout—in dooryards, road-sides, fields, waste places; general: widespread over North America.

Comments Before tea was imported from China, catnip tea was the standard beverage in England and was brought to this country by early colonists. It was also used medically. The leaves are favored by many, but not all, domestic cats and have been used as a lure for trapping wild cats such as pumas and bob-cats.

Catnip

FIGWORT FAMILY
(*Scrophulariaceae*)

Turtlehead (*Chelone glabra*)

Description Robust perennial, 1 to 3 feet tall, of grassy and brushy marshes and along streams. The erect, bluntly angled stems are often clumped and end in spikes of white flowers that are 2-lipped and 1 to 1½ inches long. As its name implies, the shape of the flower suggests the head of a turtle. Leaves are opposite, elongate, and coarsely toothed. *Summer*

Habitat and Range Minnesota: mostly in the east and north; general: temperate eastern North America.

Turtlehead

Foxglove Penstemon
(*Penstemon digitalis*)

Description Has bell-shaped white flowers, about an inch long, that are penciled inside with purple. The broad-based leaves taper to a point and are toothed. Except in the branched inflorescence, the stem is without hairs. *Spring, summer*

Habitat and Range Minnesota: rare, along eastern edge; general: eastern and central United States.

Related Species The White-flowered Penstemon (*Penstemon albidus*) is similar but has smaller white flowers in a less spreading inflorescence and stems covered with minute hairs. It is a plant of prairies and plains, and in Minnesota is found mostly in the west.

BILL JOHNSON

Foxglove Penstemon

Culver's Root
(*Veronicastrum virginicum*)

Description Erect perennial of prairies and open woods. Usually 2 to 5 feet tall, it has elongate leaves in whorls of 3 to 6, and small white flowers in tapering spikes. Each flower has 2 stamens that are longer than the petals. *Summer*

Habitat and Range Minnesota: throughout but most common on prairies in the south and west; general: temperate eastern North America.

Comments The root is somewhat poisonous and was used medicinally by Indian and pioneer doctors. One of the latter was a Dr. Culver, for whom the plant is named.

Culver's Root

RICHARD HAUG

Long-leaved Houstonia

Madder Family (*Rubiaceae*)

Long-leaved Houstonia
(*Houstonia longifolia*)

Description Low, often clumped perennial of dry, open places. Usually 4 to 8 inches tall. The flowers have 4 white or pale purple petals and are in small, spreading clusters. Stems are erect with elongate opposite leaves that are without teeth. *Spring, summer*

Habitat and Range Minnesota: widespread, usually in undisturbed, open, sandy and rocky places; general: eastern United States and adjacent Canada.

Northern Bedstraw
(*Galium boreale*)

Description Common white wildflower of late spring. It is usually 1 to 2 feet tall and grows in well-drained, open places. The small 4-petaled flowers are in a dense cluster at the top of the square stem. Leaves are elongate, without teeth, and in whorls of 4. The flowers are sweet-scented. *Spring, summer*

Habitat and Range Minnesota: throughout on prairies and brushy places, often common along roads; general: temperate North America and also in Eurasia.

Related Species There are several other species of bedstraw in Minnesota. All have whorled leaves, square stems, and small 4-petaled white flowers. Cleavers (*Galium aparine*) is a common sprawling plant of damp woods and brushy places. It clings to clothing by hooklike hairs on the stem angles.

Northern Bedstraw

Common Valerian

VALERIAN FAMILY
(*Valerianaceae*)

Common Valerian
(*Valeriana officinalis*)

Description Perennial of brushy places and swamps. It is usually 2 to 3 feet tall and has pinnately compound leaves and fibrous roots. The small white or pinkish flowers are in compact clusters at the top of the stem. They are followed by seedlike fruits ending in feathery bristles. *Summer*

Habitat and Range A native of Eurasia, it has escaped from old gardens and become naturalized here and there. In Minnesota it is occasional in the Twin Cities area and fairly common in Duluth.

Comments Valerian root contains several strong-smelling substances, including valeric acid. The dried root has been used medicinally since ancient times. Cats are attracted by its odor.

Related Species The native *Valeriana edulis*, a perennial with thick roots and a cluster of elongate basal leaves, is found in southern Minnesota prairies.

GOURD FAMILY
(*Cucurbitaceae*)

Wild Cucumber
(*Echinocystis lobata*)

Description Annual vine with square stems, deeply lobed leaves, and branched tendrils. The showy male flowers are white and in erect clusters, and the less evident female flowers are in the leaf axils. The ovoid fruits, about 2 inches long, are prickly. Eventually

Wild Cucumber

4 large black seeds are released through a hole in the lower end of the fruit, leaving behind the papery shells. Within is a 2-legged network of vascular tissue known to children as "lace pants." *Summer*

Habitat and Range Minnesota: common in moist, brushy places; general: temperate eastern North America.

Comments Also called Balsam Apple.

Wild Cucumber (fruit)

Related Species The Bur or Star Cucumber (*Sicyos angulatus*) is a fairly common herbaceous vine of moist, shady places. It has hairy stems, shallowly lobed leaves, tendrils, and burlike clusters of 1-seeded fruits.

Aster Family (*Asteraceae*)

Common Yarrow
(*Achillea millefolium*)

Description Erect, often clumped perennial with flat clusters of small white flower heads. The elongate leaves are strongly scented, nearly flat, and much divided. Plants with pink or rosy flower heads are grown in gardens and sometimes occur in the wild. *Summer*

Habitat and Range A European plant widely naturalized along roads and in old fields and pastures. In Europe it was once used for flavoring beer.

Related Species The native Western or Woolly Yarrow (*Achillea lanulosa*) is similar but has an abundance of woolly hairs on the stem. Leaf divisions stand in several planes rather than lying nearly flat. It is common throughout Minnesota on prairies and in open woods. Sometimes considered a variant (subspecies) of the Common Yarrow.

Common Yarrow

Ox-eye Daisy
(Leucanthemum vulgare)

Description The common white daisy of roadsides and old pastures. This perennial, a native of Europe, spreads by rootstocks and often grows in patches. Each slender, unbranched stem, usually 1 to 2 feet tall, ends in a flower head with a yellow center and many white rays, up to an inch long. Leaves are elongate and variously toothed and lobed. *Summer*

Habitat and Range Minnesota: widespread but most common in the northeastern third; general: throughout temperate North America.

Comments The number of rays per head varies considerably, giving rise to the petal-plucking children's game of "loves me, loves me not." Marie-Victorin, the famous French-Canadian botanist, noted that counting the rays on a large number of heads provides a useful classroom approach to the statistics of biological variation.

Ox-eye Daisy

Mayweed

Mayweed
(Anthemis cotula)

Description Low, strongly scented annual with flower heads having raised, conical centers and white rays. Leaves are much cut and divided. Usually it is less than 2 feet tall. *Summer*

Habitat and Range A weedy Eurasian species widely distributed on fertile,

DAVID CAVAGNARO

Panicled Aster

disturbed soils, such as barnyards, turkey pastures, and road shoulders along which manure has been hauled.

Comments Under the name Feverweed, this plant went west with the pioneers. An Ozark tale tells of Johnny Appleseed planting it in new settlements after his wife and child had died of "chills." Also called Dog Fennel and Dog Chamomile.

Related Species Scentless Chamomile (*Matricaria maritima*) is similar but often taller and with finely cut leaves that are nearly odorless. It also is of European origin, and in Minnesota is found in the north, especially along Lake Superior.

Panicled Aster
(*Aster lanceolatus*)

Description A common tall, white aster of drier, open marshes. It is usually 2 to 4 feet tall. The herbage is hairless or nearly so, and flower heads are about ¾ inch wide with 20 or more white rays. The stem is much branched toward the top. It may cross with goldenrods and thus is now included in the genus *Solidago*, but it looks like an aster. *Autumn*

Habitat and Range Minnesota: throughout; general: eastern and central United States and adjacent Canada.

Flat-top White Aster
(*Aster umbellatus*)

Description Stout aster of wet places. It is often 4 to 6 feet tall. Flower heads are white or cream-colored and are arranged in large,

Flat-top White Aster

flat clusters. The numerous leaves taper toward both ends. *Summer, autumn*

Habitat and Range Minnesota: throughout in marshes, brushy swamps, and roadside ditches; general: mostly eastern temperate North America.

Heath Aster (*Aster ericoides*)

Description Common white aster of dry prairies and other open places. The bushy grayish plants, usually 1 to 2 feet tall, have many small white flower heads. They are about ½ inch across and are arranged in dense, often 1-sided clusters. Heath Aster frequently grows in patches. *Autumn*

Habitat and Range Minnesota: mostly in the south and west; general: eastern and central temperate North America.

Comments Also called Frost-weed Aster.

Side-flowering Aster (*Aster lateriflorus*)

Description A robust, clumped, and much branched aster of swamp edges and brushy places. It is often as tall as 3 feet. The small white-rayed flower heads are about ½ inch across and are usually borne on one side of the upper branches. Centers of heads range from yellow to purplish, giving a "calico" effect. *Autumn*

Habitat and Range Minnesota: mostly in brushy places in the hardwood forest areas; general: temperate eastern North America.

Comments Also called Calico Aster.

Heath Aster

Side-flowering Aster

Boltonia (*Boltonia asteroides*)

Description Robust, asterlike perennial of damp prairies, swales, and edges of streams. The branched stems are often in clumps 3 to 5 feet tall. The flower heads, about 1 inch across, are numerous, have hemispherical yellow centers and narrow, usually white rays. Occasionally the rays are pale pink, purple, or blue. The seedlike fruits (achenes) differ from those of the asters and fleabanes by having no tuft of hairs at one end. *Late summer, autumn*

Habitat and Range Minnesota: mostly in south and east; general: eastern United States.

Comments Boltonia is sometimes grown in gardens.

Boltonia

Daisy Fleabane
(*Erigeron philadelphicus*)

Description Hairy plant, usually biennial, of moist meadows and roadsides. The flower heads, which are about 1 inch across, have many threadlike white, pink, or purplish rays surrounding a yellow center. The stem is erect, usually 1 to 2 feet tall, and has a tuft of slender roots at the base. The rather wide leaves clasp the stem. *Spring, summer*

Habitat and Range Minnesota: throughout; general: widely distributed in temperate North America.

Related Species The Rough Fleabane (*Erigeron strigosus*) has similar but smaller flower heads, about ½ inch across, with white rays. Stem leaves are narrow and not markedly clasping at the base. This widely distributed plant prefers dry fields and roadsides. It is usually an annual.

Daisy Fleabane

64

Plantain-leaved Everlasting
(Antennaria plantaginifolia)

Description Grayish perennial with a rosette of spoon-shaped leaves, usually 2 to 4 inches long with 3 or 5 nerves running the length of the blade. The flower heads, which have no rays and are covered with silky hairs, are clustered at the end of a slender stem. They are usually unisexual. Plants spread by runners, often forming patches. *Summer*

Habitat and Range Minnesota: dry, open places, especially in the west and south; general: eastern United States.

Related Species Several other kinds, sometimes called Ladies' Tobacco, have smaller leaves with a single midrib and are considered to be varieties of *Antennaria neglecta*. They include the Canada Everlasting, with leaves green and hairless above, and the Field Everlasting, with leaves covered on both sides by soft, gray hairs. Both form patches in pastures and other dry, open places.

Plantain-leaved Everlasting

RICHARD HAUG

Pearly Everlasting

Pearly Everlasting
(Anaphalis margaritacea)

Description Erect, often clumped perennial, usually 1 to 2 feet tall, of undisturbed open or brushy uplands. Stems and elongate leaves are woolly with white hairs. The small flower heads are clustered at the top of the stem. The tiny yellow flowers are enclosed by many white papery bracts, which might be mistaken for petals. *Summer*

Habitat and Range Minnesota: most common in the north and east, often where there have been forest fires; general: temperate North America and Asia.

Comments Pearly Everlasting is sometimes picked and dried for winter bouquets.

Sweet Everlasting
(Gnaphalium obtusifolium)

Description Erect annual, generally similar to the preceding species but with more elongate flower heads having brownish papery bracts. The herbage is fragrant. *Summer*

Habitat and Range Minnesota: mostly in the north in sandy places; general: temperate eastern North America.

Comments The Menominee burned the leaves of the plant to make sweet-scented smoke, which they used to revive people from fainting spells and to discourage ghosts that caused bad dreams.

Sweet Everlasting

RICHARD HAUG

Boneset

Boneset *(Eupatorium perfoliatum)*

Description Coarse, hairy perennial, usually 2 to 3 feet tall, with a conspicuous, flattish cluster of small white flower heads and elongate opposite leaves that are joined at the base. *Summer, autumn*

Habitat and Range Minnesota: throughout in swamps and damp pastures; general: eastern temperate North America.

Comments Boneset tea was a popular folk medicine used for diseases as diverse as common colds, malaria, and breakbone fever (dengue). This last use may account for the common name. Also called Thoroughwort.

White Snakeroot
(*Eupatorium rugosum*)

Description Perennial of shady places. The branched stems, usually 2 to 3 feet tall, bear opposite leaves with toothed, oval blades and flattish clusters of pure white flower heads. *Summer, autumn*

Habitat and Range Minnesota: mostly in hardwood forests of the south; general: eastern temperate North America.

Comments The herbage contains trematol, which is poisonous to livestock and is excreted in cow's milk. Such milk, if consumed by humans, causes "milk sickness." This is the disease from which Abraham Lincoln's mother, Nancy Hanks, died. In pioneer times cattle were often pastured in newly cleared woodlands, where Snakeroot thrives.

White Snakeroot

Rattlesnake-root
(*Prenanthes alba*)

Description Perennial of open woods and shady roadsides. It is usually 2 to 3 feet tall and has elongate clusters of nodding flower heads that are white, yellowish, or purple-tinged. Stems and leaves are bluish green. The leaves are stalked, and the leaf blades variously lobed and often widest toward the base. Bracts of the flower heads are hairless. *Summer*

Habitat and Range Minnesota: throughout, except in the southwest; general: temperate eastern North America.

EVELYN MOYLE

Rattlesnake-root

Cotton Grass

SEDGE FAMILY (*Cyperaceae*)

Cotton Grass (*Eriophorum vaginatum* var. *spissum*)

Description Clumped grasslike perennial of northern marshes, where it often grows with low shrubs. It has narrow leaves and slender triangular stems, each ending in a spikelet made conspicuous by its tuft of many long white hairs. The hairs trap heat and so promote the growth of the seeds. *Summer*

Habitat and Range Minnesota: bogs and open muskegs in the north; general: Arctic species extending south to Great Lakes region and northeastern United States.

WATER PLANTAIN FAMILY (*Alismataceae*)

Broad-leaved Arrowhead (*Sagittaria latifolia*)

Description Perennial, usually 1 to 2 feet tall, of open marshes, shores, and shallow water. The flowers have 3 white petals. Leaves are mostly basal with arrowhead-shaped blades. In late summer starchy tubers, 1 inch or more in diameter, are produced in the bottom mud. *Summer*

Habitat and Range Minnesota: throughout; general: much of North America.

Comments Also called Wapato and Duck Potato. Native Americans called them Swan Potatoes and dried them for winter food. There are several other species, some of which have elongate or elliptical

Broad-leaved Arrowhead

leaf blades. The tubers are dug and eaten by muskrats but are usually too deep in the mud for ducks.

Wild Calla

ARUM FAMILY (*Araceae*)

Wild Calla
(*Calla palustris*)

Description Perennial of swamps and quiet, shallow waters. Shiny, heart-shaped leaves are clustered at the end of the long yellow rootstock. The small flowers are crowded in a clublike spadix behind which is the elliptical white spathe. In late summer the spadix becomes a cluster of red berries. *Spring, summer*

Habitat and Range Minnesota: mostly in forested areas of the north; general: circumpolar and in North America from subarctic south to temperate regions.

Comments The plant, like most members of the arum family, contains acrid, needlelike crystals of calcium oxalate.

LILY FAMILY (*Liliaceae*)

White Camas (*Zygadenus elegans*)

Description Perennial of moist prairies and meadows. The stem, usually 1 to 2 feet tall, rises from a bulb. On it, grasslike leaves are crowded near the base. Flowers are white, tinged on the back with green, purple, or brown. They are ½ to ¾ inch across and have 6 perianth parts, each with a spotlike gland near the base. *Late spring, summer*

Habitat and Range Minnesota: prairies, mostly in the south and west; general: western North America.

Comments White Camas is poisonous to grazing animals.

White Camas

69

White Trout Lily
(Erythronium albidum)

Description Low woodland perennial with elliptical, pointed leaves that are basal and often marked with brown or purple. They are somewhat fleshy. The flower, at the end of a leafless stem, is nodding, is 1 to 2 inches across, and has 6 pointed perianth parts that are curved backward. They are white, sometimes tinged with pink or blue. *Spring*

White Trout Lily

Habitat and Range
Minnesota: most common in hardwood forests of the southeast, often growing in patches; general: temperate eastern North America.

Comments Also called Dog-tooth Violet.

Related Species The Yellow Trout Lily (*Erythronium americanum*) is similar but has yellow flowers. It is uncommon in eastern Minnesota.

Star-flowered False Solomon's Seal *(Smilacina stellata)*

Description The elongate and often arching stem bears wide leaves that taper to both ends. It terminates in a cluster of 6-parted small white flowers, each of which is connected to the stem by an unbranched stalk. The flowers are followed by berries, at first striped green and brown but red when ripe. *Spring, summer*

Habitat and Range Minnesota: open woods, prairies, and along roads and railways throughout; general: widespread in subarctic and temperate North America.

Star-flowered False Solomon's Seal

False Spikenard

Related Species Three-leaved False Solomon's Seal (*Smilacina trifolia*) has flowers and fruits similar to the Star-flowered False Solomon's Seal. However, it is a short, erect plant, about 6 inches tall, of wet woods and bogs.

False Spikenard
(Smilacina racemosa)

Description Woodland perennial with unbranched stems, often arching, usually 1 to 2 feet long. The stem bears alternate elliptical leaves and ends in a dense cluster of many small white flowers. On each inflorescence branch there are several flowers and later red berries. The stem rises from an elongate rootstock. Leaves are hairy beneath. *Late spring, summer*

Habitat and Range Minnesota: widely distributed and common in moist, rich forests; general: temperate North America, except in the Far West.

Comments The scars on the rootstock, marking the attachment position of former aerial stems, are similar to those of true Solomon's Seal (*Polygonatum*).

False Lily-of-the-valley
(Maianthemum canadense)

Description Low plant, usually 3 to 6 inches tall, of woods and woodland edges. The white flowers are in small, upright clusters. Each flower has 2 petals and 2 sepals, differing from most other monocots, which have flower parts in threes. The leaves are pointed, oval to oblong, and heart-shaped or abruptly narrowed at the base. There are usually 2 leaves on the stem, but individual leaves are also produced along the slender rootstock. The fruit is a small, pale red berry. *Spring*

False Lily-of-the-valley

Habitat and Range
Minnesota: through-
out in wooded areas;
general: temperate
eastern North
America.

Smooth Solomon's Seal (*Polygonatum biflorum*)

Description Perennial with elongate, usually arching stems, often 2 to 3 feet long. Leaves are elliptical, not hairy on the veins beneath, and arranged in 2

EVELYN MOYLE

Smooth Solomon's Seal

ranks. The small white flowers are ½ to ¾ inch long. They, and later the dark blue or black berries, hang in clusters from the leaf axils. *Late spring, summer*

Habitat and Range Minnesota: throughout in wooded areas; general: temperate eastern North America.

Comments Solomon's Seal has an ancient name. *Seal* refers to the circular scars on the rootstock where stems of former years were attached.

Related Species Hairy Solomon's Seal (*Polygonatum pubescens*) is similar but has smaller, yellowish green flowers and leaves with hairy veins beneath.

Large-flowered Trillium (*Trillium grandiflorum*)

Description Common and conspicuous spring wildflower of woods and woodland edges. The erect stems, usually about 1 foot tall, end in a whorl of 3 wide, pointed leaves and a single erect flower that has 3 white petals, 2 to 3 inches long. The flower may be pink or purple with age. The fruit is a black berry. *Spring*

Large-flowered Trillium

Habitat and Range Minnesota: moist, fertile woods in east, center, and north; general: temperate eastern North America.

Declining Trillium

Comments Also called Wake Robin.

Related Species The Snow Trillium (*Trillium nivale*) has similar upright flowers but is smaller, usually less than 6 inches tall, with petals 1 to 2 inches long. It blossoms early and is found in the southeast.

Declining Trillium
(*Trillium flexipes*)

Description The plant is much like that of the Large-flowered Trillium, but the flower is at the end of a downward-sloping stalk, 2 to 4 inches long, and is hidden beneath the leaves. The white petals are shorter than 2 inches. *Spring*

Habitat and Range Minnesota: mostly in the southern third; general: upper eastern United States.

Related Species The Nodding Trillium (*Trillium cernuum*) is similar but has a nodding flower on a short stalk, less than 1½ inches long. It is found throughout Minnesota except in some of the southwestern prairie counties.

ORCHID FAMILY (*Orchidaceae*)

White Lady's-slipper
(*Cypripedium candidum*)

Description Low lady's-slipper, usually less than 1 foot tall, with leafy stems. The flower has an inflated white lip ½ to 1 inch long that is veined with purple within. *Late spring, summer*

White Lady's-slipper

Round-leaved Orchis

Habitat and Range Minnesota: limy soils of undisturbed, moist prairies and edges of swamps in the south and west, now rare; general: from South Dakota east to the Atlantic Coast.

Comments Orchids should not be picked or transplanted and should be photographed only with great care so as not to trample or damage their growing place or neighboring orchid habitat.

Related Species The Ram's-head Lady's-slipper (*Cypripedium arietinum*) also occurs in Minnesota but is very rare. The small flower has a white lip veined with red. It grows on acid soil.

Round-leaved Orchis
(*Amerorchis rotundifolia*)

Description Low plant of moist woods and swamps. It has a single basal leaf and a leafless stalk, usually 4 to 6 inches tall, on which are several spurred flowers. The lip of the flower is white spotted with purple, and the other conspicuous flower parts are white to pale purple. *Late spring, summer*

Habitat and Range Minnesota: mostly in the north in mossy, wooded swamps, especially under white cedar and tamarack trees; general: a northern orchid ranging from Greenland, Hudson Bay, and the Yukon south to northern United States. In the far north it grows on open tundra.

Nodding Ladies' Tresses
(*Spiranthes cernua*)

Description A small but beautiful orchid of late summer and autumn. The erect stem, usually

EVELYN MOYLE

Nodding Ladies' Tresses

less than 1 foot tall, ends in a spike of small white flowers spirally arranged in 3 rows. They are markedly sweet-scented. *Late summer, autumn*

Habitat and Range Minnesota: throughout in prairies, meadows, and open forests; general: temperate eastern North America.

Related Species The Hooded Ladies' Tresses (*Spiranthes romanzoffiana*) is similar, but the side and top sepals are united to form a hood. Slender Ladies' Tresses (*Spiranthes gracilis*) is a slender-stemmed species of dry, sandy places. Its flowers are in a single spiral.

Dwarf Rattlesnake Plantain
(*Goodyera repens*)

Description Small orchid of wet, open woodlands. Usually 4 to 10 inches tall and often growing in patches. The spikes of small white flowers rise from a rosette of basal leaves, the blades of which are marked with white in a lattice pattern. *Summer*

Habitat and Range Minnesota: most common in northern and central parts; general: subarctic regions south to eastern temperate North America.

Comments Also called Lattice-leaf.

SUNDEW FAMILY
(*Droseraceae*)

Round-leaved Sundew (*Drosera rotundifolia*)

Description A small carnivorous bog plant

WELBY SMITH

Dwarf Rattlesnake Plantain

RICHARD HAUG

Round-leaved Sundew

with a somewhat contradictory way of surviving. It has both small white or pinkish flowers to attract insect pollinators in the usual way, and also leaves that lure insects (presumably a different set) to death by trap. The leaves, shaped like long-handled spoons, are covered with reddish hairs. Many of these are topped with glistening, dewlike drops that are very sticky and contain digestive enzymes. Small insects are caught in them. Other hairs, also containing digestive enzymes, fold over the insect and eventually consume it. This arrangement apparently compensates for the poor nutritional quality of the sphagnum or moist sand on which the plant usually grows. It can reproduce either by seed or by budding from detached leaves. *Summer*

Habitat and Range Minnesota: mostly in the north and east-central bogs and shores; general: circumboreal, south in North America to southern Canada, northeastern border states, and northern California.

Yellow *to* Cream
FLOWERS

Marsh Marigold
(Caltha palustris)

Description In the spring, marshes, especially along streams, may be bright with its golden yellow blossoms. The "chaliced" flowers, as Shakespeare called them, are clustered and 1 to 2 inches across. Each has 5 to 7 (often 6) showy sepals and many yellow stamens. Leaves are broadly heart-shaped or rounded and usually coarsely toothed. *Early spring*

Habitat and Range Minnesota: throughout but rare in the southwest; general: circumboreal, in North America from Arctic south to temperate United States.

Marsh Marigold

Comments *Caltha* is derived from the Latin word for "cup," and marigold probably comes from Anglo-Saxon, meaning "marsh-gold." Cattle and deer avoid eating this plant. Also called Cowslip.

Prairie Buttercup (*Ranunculus rhomboideus*)

Description Early spring perennial, 3 to 12 inches tall, with hairy stems and leaves. The lower leaves are undivided and toothed, and the flowering stem is branched. The flowers are about ¾ inch across with 5 pale yellow petals and 5 small green sepals. *Early spring*

Habitat and Range Minnesota: found mostly on dry prairies and open woods in the south and west; general: temperate eastern North America.

Related Species Early Buttercup (*Ranunculus fascicularis*) is smaller (usually less than 10 inches tall) and has spreading stems and divided leaves covered with silky hairs. Most abundant in the southern part of the state in open woods, prairies, and sunny hillsides.

Prairie Buttercup

Tall Buttercup

Tall Buttercup *(Ranunculus acris)*

Description A conspicuous annual or biennial buttercup of brushy places, pastures, fields, and roadsides. The bright yellow flowers, up to 1 inch across, are on erect, branching stems, often 2 feet tall. Leaves are deeply lobed and cut in a palmate, or "crowfoot," pattern. *Late spring*

Habitat and Range Minnesota: most common in the northeastern third; general: a European species widely naturalized in North America.

Comments The acrid juice makes it unpalatable to cattle.

Swamp Buttercup *(Ranunculus hispidus)*

Description Buttercup of moist woods, swamps, and floodplains. Flowers are bright yellow and about 1 inch across. In early spring the stem is short and erect, but later it elongates and spreads and arches. The leaves are compound with 3 stalked leaflets. *Spring, summer*

Habitat and Range Minnesota: throughout; general: temperate eastern North America.

Related Species The Yellow Water Crowfoot (*Ranunculus flabellaris*) also has yellow flowers about 1 inch across. They are on hollow stems that stand above the shallow water of ponds in springtime. The leaves are submersed and cut into many thin ribbonlike segments. This species was once abundant in prairie ponds and wetlands, which have been drained and are now fields of corn and soybeans.

Swamp Buttercup

Barberry Family
(*Berberidaceae*)

Blue Cohosh
(*Caulophylum thalictroides*)

Description Perennial of moist woods. When mature, it has a spreading, somewhat bushy appearance and is often 2 to 3 feet tall. The compound leaves have wide, thick leaflets that end in 3 or 5 blunt lobes. In spring when in flower, the developing stems and leaves are often purplish, and the clustered flowers have 6 yellow or purplish sepals. Later, globular blue berries develop, each on a thick stalk. *Spring*

Habitat and Range Minnesota: throughout, except in the northeast, mostly in hardwood forests; general: temperate North America. Also in eastern Asia.

Comments The roots, which contain glucosides, once had medicinal uses. The word *cohosh* is of Algonquian origin and means "rough."

Blue Cohosh

Blue Cohosh (fruit)

Yellow Water Lily

Water Lily Family
(*Nymphaeaceae*)

Yellow Water Lily
(*Nuphar variegatum*)

Description A common perennial aquatic plant of lakeshores and slow stretches of streams. The floating heart-shaped leaves and yellow flowers rise from a thick rootstock on the bottom. Flowers are cup-shaped and about 2 inches across, and have 5 or 6 deep yellow sepals that are often reddish at the base. There are many small fleshy petals and many stamens. The pistil matures beneath the water and

American Lotus Lily

DAVID CAVAGNARO

becomes a pod filled with large spherical seeds. These are eaten by ducks. *Summer*

Habitat and Range Minnesota: throughout; general: much of northern United States and adjacent Canada.

Comments The leaves and rootstocks are food for moose and beavers. Also called Pond Lily.

American Lotus Lily
(*Nelumbo lutea*)

Description Our largest wildflower, the pale yellow blossoms being 6 to 10 inches across when fully open. It grows in shallow water and in marshes subject to flooding. The circular leaf blade, as wide as 2 feet, has a central stalk and at first floats on the water surface. Later, both blossoms and stem rise several feet above the surface of the water. The top-shaped pod has large seeds in depressions in the upper surface. *Summer*

Habitat and Range Minnesota: shallow lakes and marshes along the Mississippi River between St. Paul and Iowa. It is also found in a few lakes in the vicinity of the Twin Cities, where it may have been planted by Native Americans, who used both the seeds and the starchy rootstocks for food; general: eastern United States.

Comments Commonly called Lotus. This species is closely related to the pink Sacred Lotus of Asia.

FUMITORY FAMILY
(*Fumariaceae*)

Golden Corydalis
(*Corydalis aurea*)

Description A low annual or biennial plant of open woods and clearings, often in sandy or rocky places. The clustered golden yellow flowers are irregularly shaped with 1 of the 4 petals ending in a blunt spur. Leaves are much divided, and the stem is often branched and spreading. Seeds are produced in curved pods. *Spring, summer*

EVELYN MOYLE

Golden Corydalis

Winter Cress

Habitat and Range Minnesota: throughout, except in the southwest; general: north-central and western United States and adjacent Canada.

Comments *Corydalis* is Greek for "horned lark."

Related Species Pale Corydalis (*Corydalis sempervirens*) has similar irregular flowers, but they are pink, tipped with yellow. Often it has sprawling stems. It grows in woods and rocky or brushy places, mostly in the north.

MUSTARD FAMILY (*Cruciferae*)

Winter Cress (*Barbarea vulgaris*)

Description A biennial mustard that flowers in spring. The plants, usually 2 to 3 feet tall, stand out as bright yellow clumps in moist meadows and fields. The small 4-petaled flowers are in elongate clusters, and the leaves and stems are hairless. Lower leaves are deeply lobed, with the end lobe the largest. *Spring*

Habitat and Range A European plant that is widely naturalized in Minnesota and elsewhere in North America.

Comments In medieval times Winter Cress was used as a poultice on wounds and was appropriately dedicated to St. Barbara, the patron saint of artillerymen. Also called Yellow Rocket.

ROSE FAMILY (*Rosaceae*)

Shrubby Cinquefoil
(*Potentilla fruticosa*)

Description Low, much branched, and often bushy shrub, up to 3 feet tall. The tough woody stems have shredded bark and bear bright yellow flowers and small pinnately compound leaves. *Summer*

Habitat and Range Minnesota: mostly in the north. Common on

Shrubby Cinquefoil

rocky headlands along Lake Superior; general: circumpolar subarctic, south in North America to northern United States. Except for its occurrence along Lake Superior, it is found only in fens and wet prairies.

Comments Shrubby Cinquefoil resists browsing, and we have seen it flourishing on heavily grazed bison ranges in parks in South Dakota and Manitoba. When grown in gardens, it is called Gold Drops.

Old Field Cinquefoil
(Potentilla simplex)

Description Perennial with slender, leafy stems that eventually elongate, become arching or trailing, and root at the ends. The palmately compound leaves have 5 leaflets. The yellow flowers are at the end of slender stalks. *Summer*

Habitat and Range Minnesota: fields, open woods, and roadsides, mostly in the south and east; general: eastern United States and adjacent Canada.

Yellow Avens
(Geum aleppicum var. strictum)

Description Perennial of moist, open or brushy places. The erect stem, usually 2 to 4 feet tall, has pinnately compound leaves with leaflets that vary considerably in shape and size. The yellow flowers, 1 to 2 inches across, have 5 petals and a cluster of long pistils in the center. These later become a spiny head of dry fruits. *Summer*

Habitat and Range Minnesota: throughout; general: temperate North America.

Old Field Cinquefoil

RICHARD HAUG

Yellow Avens

83

Bean Family (*Fabaceae*)

Partridge Pea
(*Chamaecrista fasciculata*)

Description Annual with erect stems, usually 1 to 2 feet tall. Leaves are pinnately compound with 20 to 30 leaflets, always an even number. It has yellow flowers with 5 petals of several sizes. They are followed by elongate, hairy pods. The leaves are remarkably sensitive. Leaflets fold when disturbed or when the plant is under stress in hot, dry weather. *Summer*

Habitat and Range Minnesota: mostly in the southeast in sandy, open or brushy places; general: eastern United States.

Comments Also called Sensitive Pea.

Partridge Pea

Bird's-foot Trefoil (*Lotus corniculatus*)

Description A European perennial legume that is widely established and forms showy yellow patches along highways where it is sometimes planted to control erosion. The pale green stems are sprawling and spreading. They bear leaves with 5 leaflets (the lower pair are really stipules) and rounded clusters of bright yellow flowers. Later "bird's feet" of erect, slender seed pods develop. *Summer*

Habitat and Range Minnesota: throughout but most common in the north; general: temperate eastern North America and Pacific Coast.

Bird's-foot Trefoil

84

Yellow Sweet Clover
(Melilotus officinalis)

Description A common roadside plant of European origin, usually 2 to 4 feet tall, with small yellow flowers in elongate, upright clusters. The plant is usually biennial and grows as a clump of several stems. Leaves are compound with 3 toothed leaflets. *Summer*

Habitat and Range Widely naturalized.

Comments Sometimes grown for pasture and hay.

Related Species The White Sweet Clover (*Melilotus alba*) is similar but has white flowers. It is also of European origin and widely naturalized. Both species are good

Yellow Sweet Clover

nectar sources for honeybees. Sweet clover releases the vanilla-like odor of coumarin when being dried for hay.

Wood Sorrel Family
(Oxalidaceae)

Yellow Wood Sorrel
(Oxalis stricta)

Description A common, sometimes weedy plant of open and shady places, especially where the soil has been disturbed. The leaves are compound with 3 leaflets with a notch at the end, giving them a heart-shaped appearance. The plant has a slender rootstock by which it spreads. Flowers are yellow in a loose cluster. *Summer*

Habitat and Range Widely distributed in Minnesota and throughout North America.

EVELYN MOYLE

Yellow Wood Sorrel

Comments Plants with reddish purple leaves are sometimes found. It appears that they were once planted in northern Minnesota dooryards. They still grow near old buildings. Also called Yellow Oxalis.

Leafy Spurge

EVELYN MOYLE

SPURGE FAMILY (*Euphorbiaceae*)

Leafy Spurge (*Euphorbia esula*)

Description Erect perennial, usually 1 to 2 feet tall, with leafy stems ending in conspicuous, spreading clusters of yellow "flowers." The plants spread by horizontal rootstocks and often grow in patches. Juice is milky. *Summer*

Habitat and Range Of European origin, this aggressive plant is found throughout much of North America.

Comments In Minnesota it is officially designated as a "noxious weed."

Related Species The Cypress Spurge (*Euphorbia cyparissias*) has similar "flowers" but is lower growing, usually less than 1 foot tall, and has leaves mostly less than ¼ inch wide. Once planted in dooryards and cemeteries, it persists here and there but seldom produces seeds.

ST. JOHN'S-WORT FAMILY (*Hypericaceae*)

Common St. John's-wort (*Hypericum perforatum*)

Description Clumped, much branched perennial, usually 1 to 2 feet tall. The numerous yellow flowers have 5 spreading petals and many stamens. Leaves are opposite and dotted with internal oil-filled glands. *Summer*

Habitat and Range Minnesota: mostly in the eastern portion along roads and in old pastures; general: a European species widely naturalized in North America.

Comments Common St. John's-wort can be a troublesome pasture weed, often injurious if eaten by

Common St. John's-wort

livestock. In Europe there is much folklore connected with it, including its use for treatment of weak eyes and as a talisman against thunder and witches.

Great St. John's-wort (*Hypericum pyramidatum*)

Description Robust perennial, usually 2 to 4 feet tall, of moist places, especially stream banks. The flowers are 1 to 2 inches across. They have 5 yellow petals and many conspicuous stamens. The reddish brown seed pods are about 1 inch long. Leaves are opposite and dotted internally with oil-filled glands. *Summer*

Great St. John's-wort

DAVID CAVAGNARO

Habitat and Range Minnesota: mostly in the eastern half; general: temperate eastern North America.

Comments This species has sometimes been used in folk medicine to treat respiratory troubles. There are several smaller native species.

VIOLET FAMILY (*Violaceae*)

Yellow Violet (*Viola pubescens*)

Description The common yellow violet of deep woods and wooded edges. The flowers are borne at the top of a hairy, leafy stem. There are also 1 or 2 wide-bladed basal leaves. *Spring, summer*

Habitat and Range Minnesota: throughout; general: eastern temperate North America.

Related Species The Smooth Yellow Violet (var. *eriocarpa*) is similar but is hairless or nearly so, and usually has a clump of 2 or more leafy stems and more than 2 basal leaves. It is a plant of open woods and, sometimes, of meadows.

Yellow Violet

Cactus Family
(*Cactaceae*)

Western Prickly Pear (*Opuntia macrorhiza*)

Description The sprawling, jointed stem is made up of flat sections, or "pads," armed with spines. Flowers are 2 to 3 inches across and have many pale yellow

Western Prickly Pear

petals that may be reddish at the base. There are many stamens. The fruit is fleshy. *Summer*

Habitat and Range Minnesota: open, usually rocky places in the south and west; general: central United States.

Related Species The Brittle Prickly Pear (*Opuntia fragilis*) has similar flowers, but the stem joints are long and nearly cylindrical, and the fruit is dry. It is a widely distributed western species of dry prairies and rocky places. The Purple Cactus (*Escobaria vivipara*) is found in Minnesota only near the South Dakota border.

Common Evening Primrose

Evening Primrose Family
(*Onagraceae*)

Common Evening Primrose (*Oenothera biennis*)

Description So called because the pale yellow flowers open in the evening and wither the following morning. They have 4 blunt petals that are often notched at the end. The plant is a biennial with a rosette of leaves the first year, and an erect stem, often 3 to 4 feet tall, the second year. *Summer*

Habitat and Range Minnesota: old fields, roads, and other open places, mostly in the east and north; general: temperate eastern North America.

Related Species The Rhombic Evening Primrose (*Oenothera* *rhombipetala*) of sandy areas in eastern and central Minnesota is similar but has wide petals that taper to a blunt point.

Toothed-leaved Evening Primrose (*Calylophus serrulata*)

Description Perennial of dry prairies. The somewhat woody stem, usually 1 to 2 feet tall, bears narrow leaves with widely spaced teeth. The yellow flowers are ½ to ¾ inch across. Unlike flowers of most other Evening Primroses, they remain open during the daylight hours. *Summer*

Habitat and Range Minnesota: mostly in the south and west; general: temperate western North America.

Toothed-leaved Evening Primrose

CARROT FAMILY (*Apiaceae*)

Golden Alexanders (*Zizia aurea*)

Description Late spring wildflower of open, grassy places. Perennial, usually 1 to 2 feet tall. The small yellow flowers are in a flat-topped cluster (compound umbel), and all the leaves are compound with elongate leaflets. *Spring, summer*

Habitat and Range Minnesota: moist meadows, prairies, and brushy places throughout; general: eastern United States and adjacent Canada.

Comments The name *Alexanders* is borrowed from a similar European plant.

Related Species The Heart-leaved Alexanders (*Zizia aptera*) is similar but has heart-shaped basal leaves. It grows in moist, grassy places and open woods.

Golden Alexanders

Wild Parsnip

Wild Parsnip (*Pastinaca sativa*)

Description Erect biennial, usually 2 to 4 feet tall, with flat clusters of many small yellow flowers. The leaves are pinnately compound with leaflets that are toothed and lobed. It is the wild form of the garden parsnip, but the taproot is usually woody and inedible. *Late spring, summer*

Habitat and Range A European plant frequently naturalized along roads and in waste places, especially in the vicinity of towns and farmsteads where parsnips have been raised as a vegetable.

Comments Certain individuals are sensitive to parsnips and develop dermatitis from contact with the leaves and flowers.

PRIMROSE FAMILY (*Primulaceae*)

Swamp Candles (*Lysimachia terrestris*)

Description Erect perennial of bogs and marshes. It is usually 1 to 2 feet tall. The stem bears hairless opposite leaves and 5-petaled yellow flowers in an erect, spikelike cluster. On the petals are dark markings. Reddish bulblets often develop in the leaf axils. *Summer*

Habitat and Range Minnesota: mostly in the east and north; general: temperate eastern North America.

Comments Also called Yellow or Bulb-bearing Loosestrife.

EVELYN MOYLE

Swamp Candles

Moneywort
(Lysimachia nummularia)

Description Low, trailing perennial with pale yellow flowers and nearly circular, opposite leaves. The bell-shaped flowers have 5 petals dotted with dark red. *Summer*

Habitat and Range Moneywort is a native of Europe and is widely naturalized in eastern North America.

Moneywort

Comments Moneywort was planted in pioneer gardens and in cemeteries to cover graves and is still used as ground cover in shady places. The specific name, *nummularia*, means "coinlike" and refers to the round leaves.

Fringed Loosestrife
(Lysimachia ciliata)

Description Erect, often branched perennial of damp thickets, marshes, and shores. It is usually 1 to 2 feet tall. Leaves are opposite with pointed, oval blades, and the leaf stalks are fringed on the upper angles with curly white hairs. The flowers are yellow with 5 wide, pointed petals. Each flower is on a slender stalk. *Summer*

Habitat and Range Minnesota: throughout; general: temperate North America.

Tufted Loosestrife
(Lysimachia thyrsiflora)

Description A perennial of open and wooded swamps. The erect stems, usually 1 to 2 feet tall, have elongate opposite leaves and

Fringed Loosestrife

stalked clusters or "tufts" of small yellow flowers in the leaf axils. Each flower has 5 narrow petals on which are dark markings. *Summer*

Habitat and Range Minnesota: throughout, sometimes in shallow water; general: subarctic circumpolar, in North America south to northern United States.

Prairie Loosestrife (*Lysimachia quadriflora*)

Description A midsummer perennial, about 2 feet tall, sometimes branched, growing in the moist portions of meadows, prairies, and open woods. Its clear yellow flowers are on long stalks in the axils of the leaves and are clustered near the top of the plant. The flowers are about ½ inch across, and have 5 broad, slightly pointed petals that sometimes have ragged edges. The supporting bracts are green, very narrow, and distinctly pointed. The leaves, in whorls along the stem, are stiff, unstalked, and slender, almost oblong, with smooth, rolled edges. *Summer*

Habitat and Range Minnesota: southern third and along the northwestern border; general: on prairies west of the Appalachians to Manitoba and Minnesota, and north of the Ohio River.

Tufted Loosestrife

Prairie Loosestrife

BORAGE FAMILY (*Boraginaceae*)

Carolina Puccoon (*Lithospermum caroliniense*)

Description A bright orange yellow wildflower of late spring. The erect, leafy stems, usually 1 to 2 feet tall, rise from a thick perennial root. Stems are topped by a spreading cluster of flowers. Each flower is about ¾ inch across and has 5 petals united toward

the base. Native Americans used the root to make a red dye. *Spring*

Habitat and Range Minnesota: in the southeast and center, especially on the east-central sandplain; general: much of temperate and southern United States.

Comments The word *puccoon* is of Algonquian origin, meaning "blood."

Carolina Puccoon

Related Species The Hoary Puccoon (*Lithospermum canescens*) is similar but has flowers about ½ inch across, and herbage that is densely covered with short, soft hairs. It is a fairly common plant of prairies, meadows, and open woods in Minnesota and eastern United States.

NIGHTSHADE FAMILY (*Solanaceae*)

Virginia Ground Cherry (*Physalis virginiana*)

Description Low, branched perennial, usually less than 1 foot tall, of dry, open woods, meadows, and prairies. Leaves are alternate with elongate blades. The yellow flowers have 5 spreading petals that are united at the base and have a brown center. The edible spherical fruit is enclosed in a loose, papery husk, the inflated calyx. *Summer*

EVELYN MOYLE

Virginia Ground Cherry

Habitat and Range Minnesota: mostly in the south and west; general: temperate North America.

Common Mullein

Common Mullein (*Verbascum thapsus*)

Description Robust biennial, usually 3 to 6 feet tall. During its first year, it grows as a rosette of large, soft, hairy leaves, and in its second year develops a stout, leafy stalk ending in 1 or more thick flower spikes. The pale yellow flowers open in the morning, last but a day, and are replaced the following day by others below them. The leaf hairs are branched and treelike. *Summer*

Habitat and Range A European plant widely distributed in dry, open places, especially where the soil has been disturbed.

Comments The dry spikes, soaked in tallow, were used by the Romans for torches, and the velvety leaves served the ancient Greeks as lamp wicks. Also called Flannel Plant and Aaron's Rod.

Butter-and-eggs
(*Linaria vulgaris*)

Description Upright perennial, usually 1 to 2 feet tall, of roadsides, pastures, and waste places. It often grows in patches. The stem bears many narrow leaves and ends in a cluster of conspicuous yellow flowers. The flower is 2-lipped and has a spur. An orange spot on the lower lip probably serves as a target for flying insects. *Summer*

Habitat and Range A European species widely naturalized in Minnesota and elsewhere in North America.

Comments It is quite ornamental and was planted in pioneer gardens. Also called Toadflax.

Butter-and-eggs

Common Lousewort
(Pedicularis canadensis)

Description Low, hairy perennial, usually 6 to 12 inches tall, of dry meadows, prairies, and upland woods. The elongate leaves have many side lobes. Flowers are 2-lipped, commonly yellow, and in dense clusters. *Summer*

Habitat and Range Minnesota: mostly in the south and west; general: temperate eastern North America.

Comments Both the common and generic names refer to the ancient belief that cattle become lousy by feeding on lousewort. Also called Wood Betony.

Common Lousewort

Related Species The Swamp Lousewort (*Pedicularis lanceolata*) is similar but taller and with pale yellow or nearly white flowers. It grows in wet, open places.

BLADDERWORT FAMILY
(Lentibulariaceae)

Greater Bladderwort
(Utricularia vulgaris)

Description A remarkable, carnivorous aquatic plant of quiet, shallow waters. The elongate stems float just beneath the water surface and have much divided, submerged leaves on which are tiny bladderlike traps that capture and digest minute aquatic animals. In summer, short, leafless stems emerge from the water. Each bears 2-lipped yellow flowers, about 1 inch long. The flower has a short spur at its base. *Summer*

Greater Bladderwort

RICHARD HAUG

Habitat and Range Minnesota: throughout in shallow, undisturbed waters; general: circumpolar, in North America from subarctic to southern United States and Mexico.

Yellowish Gentian

GENTIAN FAMILY (*Gentianaceae*)

Yellowish Gentian (*Gentiana alba*)

Description Perennial with upright stems, 1 to 2 feet tall, ending in a cluster of greenish white to yellowish white flowers, 1 to 1½ inches long. The opposite leaves have 3 nerves, are stalkless, and somewhat clasp the stem. *Autumn*

Habitat and Range Minnesota: uncommon and local, mostly in the southeast; general: eastern United States and adjacent Canada.

ASTER FAMILY (*Asteraceae*)

Common Sunflower (*Helianthus annuus*)

Description Robust, usually branched annual of dry, open places. Commonly 2 to 5 feet tall with flower heads 3 to 6 inches across. The center or the head (disk) is brown or purple. Leaves are coarsely toothed and often heart-shaped. *Summer, autumn*

Habitat and Range Minnesota: throughout, often on disturbed soil along roads; general: temperate North America but most common in the west. This plant is the ancestor of the cultivated sunflower.

Related Species The Stiff Sunflower (*Helianthus laetiflorus*) also has heads with dark disks. It is a prairie perennial, often growing on sandy soils. Stems are slender and wiry and usually 2 to 4 feet tall. The opposite leaves are rough and mostly 3-nerved.

Jerusalem Artichoke (*Helianthus tuberosus*)

Description Robust perennial sunflower, often 5 to 8 feet tall. The heads have yellow disks, and the leaf blades are less than 3 times as long as broad. Gnarled tubers are produced at the base of the stem. *Summer, autumn*

Habitat and Range Minnesota: throughout on upland soils but most common in the south

Common Sunflower

Jerusalem Artichoke

and west; general: temperate eastern North America west to the Rocky Mountains.

Comments The tubers were eaten by Native Americans and are still raised for food. They are of value for special diets since they contain inulin, not starch.

Related Species Two other perennial sunflowers are similar but have narrow leaves. Both thrive in wet places. The Giant Sunflower (*Helianthus giganteus*) is most common in the north. Stems are hairy below the inflorescence, and the leaves usually have few teeth. The Sawtooth Sunflower (*Helianthus grosseserratus*), which is most common in the south, has hairless stems and usually coarsely toothed leaves.

Maximilian's Sunflower
(*Helianthus maximiliani*)

Description A prairie perennial, usually 3 to 5 feet tall. The elongate, keeled, and arching leaves are rough with short hairs. The disk of the flower head is yellow. *Summer, autumn*

Habitat and Range Prairies and plains of Minnesota and central North America, often on sandy soil.

Comments This sunflower is named after Prince Maximilian of Wied, Germany, who early in the nineteenth century traveled the plains with artist Carl Bodmer, known for his paintings of Native Americans and western scenery.

Maximilian's Sunflower

Ox-eye (*Heliopsis helianthoides*)

Description Perennial, usually 1 to 3 feet tall, with stiff, erect stems, sunflower-like heads, and opposite leaves that have wide, toothed blades. Heads are usually about 2 inches across and have raised centers. The yellow rays remain attached to the head after withering. *Spring, summer*

Ox-eye

Habitat and Range Minnesota: throughout on prairies, roadsides, and in open woods; general: much of temperate North America.

Comments There are double cultivars that resemble a yellow zinnia.

Brown-eyed Susan

Brown-eyed Susan (*Rudbeckia hirta*)

Description A common, bright summer wildflower of roadsides and fields. The slender, erect stems are usually 1 to 2 feet tall. They end in flower heads that have raised, rounded centers that are purplish brown and surrounded by yellow rays. Occasionally the rays are brown at the base. Leaves are elongate, without lobes, and frequently have 3 nerves. *Summer*

Habitat and Range Minnesota: throughout, often on sandy soil; general: temperate eastern North America.

Wild Golden Glow (*Rudbeckia laciniata*)

Description A robust and usually clumped perennial, often 5 to 8 feet tall, with large lower leaves that are lobed or divided. Flower heads are 2 to 3 inches across. They have drooping yellow rays and raised greenish centers. *Summer*

Habitat and Range Minnesota: most common in the southeast in moist, often brushy places; general: temperate eastern North America.

Comments Also called Green-headed Coneflower.

Related Species A double variety, the Garden Golden Glow, is sometimes established along roads near old gardens and dwellings. This is the only instance we know of in which the name of the wild plant is derived from the garden variety.

EVELYN MOYLE

Wild Golden Glow

Gray-headed Coneflower
(*Ratabida pinnata*)

Description Perennial of open places and edges of woods. The showy flower heads have drooping yellow rays and raised grayish centers that are shorter than the rays. Both the erect stems, commonly 1 to 3 feet tall, and the divided leaves are covered with short gray hairs. *Summer*

Habitat and Range Minnesota: mostly in the south, where it is often common along roads and railways; general: temperate eastern North America.

Related Species The Long-headed Coneflower (*Ratabida columnifera*) is similar, but the flower heads have a dark, columnar center longer than the rays. Rays are usually yellow but may be partly or wholly purple. A plant of western dry prairies and plains; in Minnesota in the south and west.

Gray-headed Coneflower

Stiff Tickseed
(Coreopsis palmata)

Description Perennial. Early summer wildflower of open places. The stiff, erect stems, usually 1 to 2 feet tall, end in flower heads about 1½ inches across. They have 6 to 10 yellow rays, each ending in 3 blunt teeth. Leaves are opposite and have 3 elongate lobes. The stems rise from running rootstocks and often are in patches. *Early summer*

Habitat and Range Minnesota: well-drained prairies and open woods in the south, often common along railways; general: central North America from Manitoba to Texas.

Stiff Tickseed

Nodding Beggar's-ticks
(Bidens cernua)

Description Annual, usually 1 to 2 feet tall, of wet places such as marshes and pond margins. The small, sunflower-like heads have 6 to 8 yellow rays and are nodding when in fruit. Bases of the opposite leaves are often joined. The elongate, flat fruits end in 2 to 4 barbed awns, which stick tightly to clothing and fur. *Autumn*

Nodding Beggar's-ticks

Habitat and Range Widespread in Minnesota, temperate North America, and Eurasia.

Comments Also called Bur Marigold and Stick-tight.

Cup Plant
(Silphium perfoliatum)

Description Stout perennial, usually 3 to 6 feet tall, with sunflower-like heads up to 4 inches across. Stems are square, and the wide opposite

RICHARD HAUG

Cup Plant

leaves are united at the base to form a "cup." The heads are arranged in a spreading cluster and have 20 to 30 yellow rays. *Summer, autumn*

Habitat and Range Minnesota: on moist, fertile soils, especially in river valleys in the south, but not common; general: temperate eastern North America.

Comments The flower heads of *Silphium* have fertile, seed-producing ray flowers and sterile disk flowers. In sunflowers (*Helianthus*) the opposite is true.

Compass Plant
(*Silphium laciniatum*)

Description Among the tallest of our nonwoody plants, often reaching a height of 6 to 8 feet. This typical prairie perennial has flower heads with yellow rays much like those of sunflowers. They are usually 3 to 4 inches across. The large hairy leaves are deeply cut and divided. *Summer, autumn*

Habitat and Range Minnesota: mostly in the south on undisturbed prairie remnants; general: eastern United States but now rare.

Comments When Compass Plant grows in dry, open places, the lower leaves often stand on edge and are oriented in a north-south direction, hence its name. Resinous material collects where a stem is broken. This was chewed by pioneer children. The plant is highly palatable to cattle and easily destroyed by grazing. Also called Rosinweed.

EVELYN MOYLE

Compass Plant

Sneezeweed

Sneezeweed
(Helenium autumnale)

Description Perennial, usually 2 to 4 feet tall, with elongate leaves, the bases of which extend down the stem as flanges or wings. The numerous flower heads have raised, nearly globular centers and wedge-shaped yellow rays that end in 3 coarse teeth. Often the stems are clumped. *Summer, autumn*

Habitat and Range Widespread in moist, open places in Minnesota and elsewhere in temperate North America. It often grows along streams.

Comments The flowers release a volatile oil that has insecticidal properties. The Menominee used the dried flower heads to promote sneezing to loosen a head cold. There are garden cultivars, called Helen's Flower, with yellow to brick red flowers.

Tansy *(Tanacetum vulgare)*

Description A European perennial once grown as a flavoring and medicinal plant. The stems, usually 2 to 4 feet tall and often in clumps or patches, are topped by flat clusters of rayless yellow flower heads. The elongate, much divided leaves are strongly scented and bitter. *Summer*

Habitat and Range Widely naturalized in Minnesota and elsewhere in temperate North America, especially along roads and in old fields and dooryards.

Comments Tansy was once used in cooking and cheese making, and as a tonic tea. It can be poisonous, however, if too much is used.

Tansy

Prairie Ragwort
(Senecio plattensis)

Description Prairie perennial, usually 1 to 2 feet tall, with a spreading cluster of small flower heads, each having yellow rays and a cuplike involucre composed of a single row of narrow green bracts. The basal leaves are stalked and toothed, and the narrower stem leaves are often irregularly toothed and lobed. Stems and leaves are woolly with soft white hairs. *Late spring, summer*

Habitat and Range Minnesota: dry prairies, mostly in the south and west; general: central and western temperate North America.

Related Species Balsam Ragwort *(Senecio pauperculus)* is a similar but less woolly plant of northern woods and sandy places. Golden Ragwort *(Senecio aureus)* grows on

Prairie Ragwort

wet soil. Its flowers are similar to those of Prairie Ragwort, but the basal leaves are heart-shaped and toothed, and have a marked balsamic odor when crushed.

Golden Aster
(Heterotheca villosa)

Description Branched, often clumped and bushy perennial, usually 1 to 2 feet tall, of dry, open places. The flower heads are about 1 inch across and have yellow rays. Leaves and stems are hairy. *Summer, autumn*

Habitat and Range Minnesota: prairies and brushy places, often on sand, most common in the west and center; general: upper Midwest and Great Plains.

Golden Aster

Gum Plant
(Grindelia squarrosa)

Description Glabrous biennial or perennial of open places and coarse soils. The erect, often clumped stems are commonly 1 to 3 feet tall, and the yellow-rayed flower heads are about 1 inch across. The narrow involucre bracts beneath the rays are backward-curved and sticky with a resinous, odorous gum. Leaves are elongate and usually toothed. *Summer, autumn*

Gum Plant

Stiff Goldenrod

Habitat and Range Widely distributed, especially along roads and railways in Minnesota and elsewhere in North America.

Comments Also called Gum-weed.

Stiff Goldenrod (Solidago rigida)

Description Flower heads are in a wide, flat or somewhat rounded cluster that is several inches across. Stems are often clumped and commonly 2 to 4 feet tall. The oval to oblong stem leaves and the stalked basal leaves are rough with short, stiff hairs. *Summer, autumn*

Habitat and Range Minnesota: prairies and roadsides, especially in the south and west; general: temperate North America.

Comments Goldenrods are perennials that bloom in late summer and autumn. All have small heads of yellow flowers and alternate stem leaves.

Grass-leaved Goldenrod
(Euthamia graminifolia)

Description Flower heads are in a loose, flattish cluster. The stems, usually 1 to 2 feet tall, are branched upward and have elongate, narrow leaves, usually with 3 parallel veins (nerves). *Summer, autumn*

Habitat and Range Minnesota: open and brushy places, often on sandy soil; general: temperate North America.

Zigzag Goldenrod
(Solidago flexicaulis)

Description Woodland goldenrod with erect, somewhat zigzag stems. The pointed, oval leaves are coarsely toothed. Flower heads are in small, often stalked clusters at the base of the upper leaves. *Summer, autumn*

Habitat and Range Minnesota: woods and woodland edges, especially in hardwood forest areas; general: temperate eastern North America.

Showy Goldenrod
(Solidago speciosa)

Description Flower heads are in a blunt, plumelike cluster that has ascending (not arching) side branches. Stems are usually clumped, 1 to 3 feet tall, and the herbage is nearly hairless. One of the most beautiful goldenrods. *Summer, autumn*

Habitat and Range Minnesota: prairies and open woods, especially in the south and west, often on sandy soil; general: eastern and central United States.

Grass-leaved Goldenrod

Zigzag Goldenrod

Showy Goldenrod

Related Species
The Hairy Goldenrod (*Solidago hispida*) also has a blunt inflorescence with ascending branches. However, the inflorescence is narrow. Flower heads are usually orange yellow, and the herbage is hairy. It grows in dry sandy and rocky places throughout Minnesota.

Canada Goldenrod
(*Solidago canadensis*)

Description Common roadside and pasture goldenrod. Its plumes of yellow flower heads nod at the tip and have arching side branches. Stems are commonly 2 to 4 feet tall and grow in clumps or patches. The upper leafy part of the stem is hairy. The leaves decrease gradually in size upward on the stem, are coarsely toothed, and have 3 main veins (nerves). *Summer, autumn*

Habitat and Range Minnesota: throughout; general: temperate North America.

Comments Both this species and Late Goldenrod often have a rounded swelling (gall) on the stem, caused by an insect. The fly grub the galls contain are used for winter fishing bait.

Related Species Late Goldenrod (*Solidago gigantea*) is similar but more robust, often as tall as 5 or 6 feet. Stems are hairless and usually shiny and reddish. It is most common in moist, open places.

Gray Goldenrod
(*Solidago nemoralis*)

Description Low, slender goldenrod, usually not taller than 2 feet,

Canada Goldenrod

EVELYN MOYLE

Gray Goldenrod

of prairies and dry roadsides. It has ashy gray herbage and basal leaves markedly larger than the stem leaves. The cluster of flower heads nods and is somewhat 1-sided. *Summer, autumn*

Habitat and Range
Common on dry, open places in Minnesota and elsewhere in temperate western North America.

Missouri Goldenrod
(*Solidago missouriensis*)

Description Low-growing and early flowering goldenrod of prairies. It is usually 1 to 2 feet tall. Stem leaves are narrow, toothed, and firmly erect. The herbage, including the bracts of the flower heads, is smooth and hairless. Leaves are markedly 3-nerved. The large basal leaves are usually gone at the time of flowering. *Summer, early autumn*

Habitat and Range
Minnesota: prairies in south and west; general: typical goldenrod of the Great Plains.

Related Species
The Early Goldenrod (*Solidago juncea*) is quite similar but is a plant of northern forest openings and roadsides, especially on sandy soil. Often blossoms in July. The inflorescence is nodding and about as wide as long. Usually there is a tuft of large, rather soft basal leaves that are somewhat 3-nerved.

Missouri Goldenrod

107

Common Dandelion

Common Dandelion
(Taraxacum officinale)

Description One of our persistent companions. It thrives despite being stepped on, mowed, or grazed, and soon returns after being decimated with herbicides. Leaves of the flat rosette have backward-pointing teeth: in French, *dent de lion*; hence the name. They rise from a taproot. The yellow flower heads open in the morning and close in the evening. They attract bees and other insects but can set fruits without pollination. The tawny or pale brown fruits (achenes) are wind-borne on silken parasols. *Spring, summer*

Habitat and Range This European species is widely distributed in North America.

Related Species
The Red-seeded Dandelion (*Taraxacum erythrospermum*) is similar but usually somewhat smaller. It has deeply cut leaves and reddish brown "seeds." It is also Eurasian and widespread.

Common Sow Thistle
(Sonchus uliginosus)

Description An erect perennial with stems usually 2 to 4 feet tall and yellow flower heads resembling but usually somewhat larger than those of dandelions. The elongate leaves are lobed and have weak prick-

Common Sow Thistle

les. The juice is milky, and the plant spreads by rootstocks, often forming patches. *Summer*

Habitat and Range A European plant widely distributed in North America, especially along roads. Before modern herbicides were used, it was a persistent weed of grain fields and difficult to control. In the Red River valley fields were once yellow with its blossoms.

Prickly Lettuce (*Lactuca serriola*)

Description Weedy annual or biennial that is probably the ancestor of cultivated lettuce. The erect and branched stem, usually 2 to 3 feet tall, bears numerous small, pale yellow flower heads and elongate leaves with weak prickles. The seedlike gray fruits become windborne by a tuft of silky hairs. *Summer*

Prickly Lettuce

Habitat and Range A European species that is widely distributed in North America.

Comments In spring, when only basal leaves are present, these may turn on edge and become oriented in a north-south direction to form a "compass plant."

Canada Lettuce (*Lactuca canadensis*)

Description Native annual or biennial, sometimes growing to 6 feet. It has numerous small, deep yellow flower heads and seedlike, nearly black

Canada Lettuce

Goat's Beard

achenes. Leaves are elongate and lobed or toothed but not prickly. *Summer*

Habitat and Range Minnesota: throughout in well-drained open and brushy places; general: temperate eastern North America.

Goat's Beard
(*Tragopogon dubius*)

Description Common biennial of roadsides. The erect stems, 1 to 3 feet tall, end in pale yellow flower heads much like those of a large dandelion. They have long green bracts standing behind the shorter, yellow rays. The flower heads face the sun. Leaves are elongate, parallel-veined, and without teeth or lobes. *Spring, summer*

Habitat and Range This European plant is widely naturalized in North America.

Comments The rounded heads of parachute-winged fruits are sometimes gathered for winter bouquets after being sprayed with thin lacquer to fix the fruits in place. Goat's Beard is one of the few dicots that have parallel-veined leaves. The juice is milky.

Pale Agoseris (*Agoseris glauca*)

Description Perennial of moist prairies. It has dandelion-like yellow flower heads at the end of slender, leafless stalks. The leaves are basal, elongate, and mostly without teeth or lobes. They have parallel veins. The plant is often pale bluish green and has milky juice. *Summer*

Habitat and Range Minnesota: prairies, mostly in the west;

Goat's Beard (fruit)

general: prairies of western North America.

Comments Also called Prairie Dandelion and False Dandelion.

Kalm's Hawkweed
(Hieracium kalmii)

Description Perennial, 1 to 3 feet tall, of open woods and fields. The leafy stem ends in an open cluster of dandelion-like, deep yellow flower heads, each about 1 inch across. Leaves are elongate and usually have a few coarse teeth. *Summer*

Habitat and Range Minnesota: mostly in the north and east in sandy areas; general: temperate North America.

Pale Agoseris

Comments The genus *Hieracium* is extremely complex, and species can be told apart only by a very close examination of the flower. *Hieracium kalmii* is frequently confused with Canada Hawkweed (*Hieracium canadense*).

Hawk's-beard
(Crepis tectorum)

Description
A slender-stemmed annual, usually 1 to 2 feet tall, with narrow, elongate leaves or leaf segments. It has spreading clusters of pale yellow flower heads, each about ½ inch across. The seed-like achenes are tipped

Kalm's Hawkweed

with a tuft of white hairs. *Summer*

Habitat and Range Minnesota: open, disturbed soils throughout; general: this and several quite similar European species are widely distributed in North America, mostly as weedy plants. *Crepis tectorum* has become common in Minnesota in recent years.

LILY FAMILY
(*Liliaceae*)

Clintonia
(*Clintonia borealis*)

Description Perennial of damp woods and swampy, brushy places. It is usually less than 1 foot tall and has a basal clump of 3 to 5 shiny, elliptical leaves. A spreading cluster of 6-parted, pale yellow flowers is borne at the top of a slender, leafless stem. Leaf margins have silky white hairs. The flowers are followed by spherical blue berries, about ⅓ inch across. *Spring, summer*

Habitat and Range Minnesota: mostly in the coniferous forest region of the north; general: temperate eastern North America.

Comments The Menominee placed the leaves on dog bites to "draw out the poison," and Ojibwe women made artistic patterns by biting the leaf blades. Also called Blue-bead Lily.

EVELYN MOYLE

Hawk's-beard

Clintonia

Large-flowered Bellwort
(*Uvularia grandiflora*)

Description Spring perennial of moist woods. Blossoming clumps are usually less than 1 foot tall, but later the forking stem lengthens. The 6-parted, pale yellow flower is nodding and 1 to 2 inches long. Perianth parts are often twisted. Leaves have the stem passing through them near the base. The fruit is a capsule containing seed. *Spring*

Habitat and Range Minnesota: throughout in wooded areas but not in the southwest; general: temperate eastern North America.

Large-flowered Bellwort

Sessile-leaved Bellwort
(*Uvularia sessilifolia*)

Description Woodland perennial, with leafy stems less than 10 inches long. It often spreads by rootstocks to form patches. The elongate leaves taper to both ends and have no stalks. Flowers are nodding, 6-parted, and ½ to 1 inch long. They are pale yellow or cream. The fruit is a 3-sided pod. *Spring*

Habitat and Range Minnesota: throughout except in the southwestern and extreme western prairie region; general: temperate eastern North America.

Comments Also called Wild Oats.

AMARYLLIS FAMILY
(*Amaryllidaceae*)

Yellow Star Grass
(*Hypoxis hirsuta*)

Description In late spring some meadows are starred with its bright yellow flowers. This plant, usually shorter than 8 inches, has grassy

Sessile-leaved Bellwort

Yellow Star Grass

leaves on which are soft hairs. The leaves and slender stem rise from a small corm. Flowers are in a few-flowered umbel. Each has 6 perianth parts and is ½ to ¾ inch wide. *Spring, summer*

Habitat and Range Minnesota: throughout in damp meadows and prairies, except in the northeast; general: temperate eastern North America.

Iris Family (*Iridaceae*)

Yellow Flag (*Iris pseudacorus*)

Description Robust perennial of wet places; often 3 to 4 feet tall. The clumped basal leaves are erect and swordlike, and the large, pale yellow flowers are on a branched, flowering stem. *Spring, early summer*

Habitat and Range A native of Europe that came to America as a garden plant but has become widely naturalized in eastern temperate North America. In Minnesota, plants that have escaped culti-vation are found occasionally in marshes and along lakeshores and streams.

Comments Yellow Flag grows along the River Lys in Flanders, and because of this, Marie-Victorin, French Canadian botanist, considered it to be the original model for the fleur-de-lis of French heraldry.

Orchid Family (*Orchidaceae*)

Yellow Lady's-slipper (*Cypripedium calceolus* var. *parviflorum*)

Description Leafy-stemmed lady's-slipper, up to 2 feet tall, with flowers having an inflated yellow lip. There are two American varieties: the Large Yellow

Yellow Flag

Lady's-slipper (var. *pubescens*) has a lip, or "slipper," usually 1¼ to 2 inches long, and purple brown sepals; the Small Yellow Lady's-slipper (var. *parviflorum*) has a shorter lip and brownish yellow sepals. The former is most common in woods, especially hardwood forests, and the latter in swamps and along shores. In the far north they may grow in the same areas, and it may be harder to separate their identities. *Late spring, summer*

Yellow Lady's-slipper

Habitat and Range Minnesota: occasional throughout, except in the southwest; general: much of United States and adjacent Canada. Also in Eurasia.

Early Coral Root
(Corallorhiza trifida)

Description An abundant small orchid living in partnership with soil fungi, often in boggy woods and swamps. It may grow singly or in clumps from a mass of coral-like root stalks. The erect stem, 4 to 12 inches high, is greenish yellow and bare except for 1 or more overlapping sheaths. It ends in an elongate cluster of small greenish yellow flowers with 6 "petals," the lowest of which is modified to form a white lip sometimes dotted with purple. The small seed capsules droop when ripe. *Spring, early summer*

Habitat and Range Minnesota: wooded areas of center and north; general: Arctic America south through northern border states in cool areas.

Early Coral Root

Orange
FLOWERS

TOUCH-ME-NOT FAMILY (*Balsaminaceae*)

Spotted Touch-me-not (*Impatiens capensis*)

Spotted Touch-me-not

Description Annual, often 2 to 3 feet tall, of damp places. The stems are watery, and the leaves oval and coarsely toothed. The orange yellow flower, commonly dotted with reddish brown, has a curved, forward-pointing spur and hangs, nicely balanced, on a slender stalk. When the mature seed capsule is touched, it explodes into curling segments, scattering the seeds. *Summer*

Habitat and Range Minnesota: throughout; general: temperate eastern and central North America.

Comments Also called Spotted Jewelweed.

Butterflyweed

Related Species Pale Touch-me-not (*Impatiens pallida*) is similar, but the base color of the flower is pale yellow, and the short spur is downward pointing. In Minnesota it grows mostly in moist places in the south.

MILKWEED FAMILY (*Asclepiadaceae*)

Butterflyweed (*Asclepias tuberosa*)

Description One of the brightest and most conspicuous of northern wildflowers. Stems, usually 1 to 2 feet tall, are often clumped and bear narrow alternate leaves and spreading clusters (umbels) of flowers ranging from bright yellow to blazing orange. Herbage is hairy. This plant, unlike other milkweeds, has no milky juice. *Late spring, summer*

Habitat and Range Minnesota: mostly in the south and east in open places, often on sand; general: eastern and central North America.

Comments Butterflyweed makes a showy garden perennial and can be raised from seed or

Orange Hawkweed

root cuttings. The thick root was used in Native American and folk medicine, especially for lung and chest complaints. Also called Pleurisy Root.

ASTER FAMILY (*Asteraceae*)

Orange Hawkweed
(*Hieracium aurantiacum*)

Description Low perennial, usually less than 1 foot tall. The hairy, leafless stem is topped by a spreading cluster of bright red orange flower heads, each about ¾ inch across. Leaves are elliptical and in a basal cluster. The plants spread by rootstocks and runners and often grow in patches. *Summer*

Habitat and Range Minnesota: most common in the northeast, where it forms red orange patches along roads and in clearings; general: naturalized here and there throughout temperate North America. Often considered a weed. In Eurasia it is an alpine plant.

Comments Also called King-devil and Devil's Paintbrush.

LILY FAMILY (*Liliaceae*)

Tawny Day Lily
(*Hemerocallis fulva*)

Description Perennial of roads and open places, especially near old home sites. The large tawny orange flowers, about 4 inches long, are at the end of a leafless stalk. They last but a single day and do not produce seeds. The clumped basal leaves are keeled and somewhat arching. There is a clump of thick roots, and the plants spread by short rootstocks to form patches. *Summer*

Habitat and Range This native of eastern Asia was imported as a gar-

Tawny Day Lily

den plant. It is widely naturalized in North America. The double form, var. *kwanso*, has also escaped from gardens.

Comments In China the flower buds are used in cooking. It is likely that Day Lily has been spread along highways by road maintenance equipment.

Turk's-cap Lily
(*Lilium michiganense*)

Description A beautiful wild-flower. The erect stem, usually 3 to 5 feet tall, rises from a scaly bulb. It has several whorls of leaves and 1 or more conspicuous, nodding flowers, each with 6 backward-curving perianth parts, 3 petals, and 3 sepals. They are yellow to orange red, dotted with purple, and about 3 inches across. *Summer*

Turk's-cap Lily

Habitat and Range Minnesota: damp meadows, roadsides, and brushy places; widespread but mostly in the east; general: temperate eastern North America.

Comments The Turk's-cap Lily is now uncommon, largely because of farming of meadows and careful maintenance of roadsides.

Wood Lily (*Lilium philadelphicum*)

Description The orange red flowers are erect and top the stem, which is usually 1 to 2 feet tall. Leaves are scattered along the stem, except the uppermost, which are whorled. Flowers are 2 to 3 inches across and spotted inside with purple. *Summer*

Habitat and Range Minnesota: throughout in open and brushy places but most common in the pine forest country of the north; general: temperate North America.

Wood Lily

Pink *to* Red

FLOWERS

CROWFOOT FAMILY (*Ranunculaceae*)

Columbine (*Aquilegia canadensis*)

Description A graceful, usually clumped wild-flower of open woods and brushy and rocky places. It commonly grows 1 to 3 feet tall and has compound basal and stem leaves. The nod-ding flower has 5 scarlet sepals ending in long spurs, and between them 5 spreading yellow petals. Shiny, black seeds are produced in a cluster of erect pods. *Spring*

Habitat and Range Minnesota: throughout; general: temperate eastern and central North America.

Comments *Columbine* refers to the resemblance of the flowers to a flock of doves, and *Aquilegia* likens the spurs to claws of eagles. Both avian analogies are more applicable to the short-spurred European columbine than to ours. The flowers are visited by hummingbirds and long-tongued sphinx moths. Also called Honeysuckle.

Columbine

MUSTARD FAMILY (*Cruciferae*)

Sweet Rocket
(*Hesperis matronalis*)

Description Robust biennial, usu-ally 3 to 4 feet tall, which has long been grown in gardens and often escapes to shady spots along roads. The flowers are usually deep pur-ple but may be white or shades between. They have 4 petals, are about an inch across, and are markedly sweet scented in the evening. The herbage is covered with soft hairs. *Spring*

Habitat and Range A native of Europe widely established throughout eastern North America.

Comments Also called Dame's Violet.

Sweet Rocket

ROSE FAMILY (*Rosaceae*)

Smooth Wild Rose
(*Rosa blanda*)

Description The most common of four roses native to Minnesota. Grows to 6 feet high and has few or no bristles on the upper main stem and side branches, and none on the new growth. The flowers open in clusters of 1 to 4. Widespread and common in open and brushy areas. *Summer*

Habitat and Range Minnesota: throughout; general: northern temperate North America.

Comments Wild rose hips are edible and are high in vitamin C. The flowers provide pollen but no nectar for bees.

Smooth Wild Rose

Related Species Prickly Wild Rose (*Rosa acicularis*) is a robust wild rose common in the northern forested part of the state. The prickly, often arching stems are about 3 feet tall. Flowers mostly open singly and are scattered over the bush. Prairie Wild Rose (*Rosa arkansana*) is a smaller (usually less than 1½ feet tall) wild rose of the prairies in the south and west. The erect woody stems are covered with bristles and topped with a cluster of pink or rosy flowers.

Marsh Cinquefoil
(*Potentilla palustris*)

Description Erect reddish plant of marshes and bogs, sometimes with the lower parts growing in water. The stem, 1 to 3 feet tall, ends in a loose cluster of reddish purple flowers and has pinnately compound leaves. *Summer*

Habitat and Range Minnesota: most common in the north; general: circumpolar subarctic, ranging south in North America to northern United States.

C. COLSTON BURRELL

Marsh Cinquefoil

Purple Avens
(Geum triflorum)

Description This low reddish plant of prairies is usually less than 1 foot tall and grows in clumps or patches. The elongate leaves are pinnately compound, with many leaflets that are toothed and covered with soft hairs. The nodding flowers have conspicuous red purple sepals. After flowering, the styles elongate to form an erect brush of soft, slender plumes, the "Prairie Smoke." *Spring, summer*

Purple Avens

Habitat and Range Minnesota: prairies, mostly in the south and west; general: temperate central and western North America.

Comments A tea was made from its roots by Native Americans. Also called Prairie Smoke.

BEAN FAMILY (*Fabaceae*)

Red Clover (*Trifolium pratense*)

Description A robust clover, usually 1 to 2 feet tall, with hairy stems and rounded heads of rosy red flowers. There is often a dark spot on the leaflets of the compound leaves. The flowers are usually pollinated by bumblebees. *Spring, summer*

Habitat and Range This native of Eurasia is sometimes grown for forage and is widely naturalized in North America.

Related Species Rabbit's-foot Clover (*Trifolium arvense*), also

Red Clover

from Europe, is an annual with hairy stems and elongate, silky gray heads of white or pink flowers. It grows on road shoulders and in sandy fields.

Crown Vetch
(Coronilla varia)

Description Perennial with spreading, sprawling stems, pinnately compound leaves, and pink and white flowers in rounded crownlike clusters. *Summer*

Habitat and Range A native of Europe, Asia, and North Africa. It is widely established in eastern North America and often crowds out native plants.

Crown Vetch

Comments It is planted to control soil erosion along highways. In early summer roadside bank cuts may be pink with the numerous flowers.

Pointed-leaved Tick Trefoil *(Desmodium glutinosum)*

Description Summer wildflower of woods and woodland edges. Usually 2 to 3 feet tall, the upright stem bears a cluster of large compound leaves, each with 3 leaflets. Above these are slender, flowering stalks with many pink or purplish flowers. Flowers are followed by flat, jointed pods covered with tiny hooked hairs. The pods break into segments when mature and adhere to clothing and fur. *Summer*

Habitat and Range Minnesota: mostly in the southern half in hardwood forests; general: temperate eastern North America.

Pointed-leaved Tick Trefoil

Canada Tick Trefoil
(Desmodium canadense)

Description Robust, erect, and often clumped perennial of dry, open, and brushy places. Usually 3 to 4 feet tall. The purplish red flowers are in elongate clusters that are branched and somewhat leafy. Stems and compound leaves are hairy. Pods are similar to those of the preceding species. *Summer*

Habitat and Range Minnesota: throughout except in the northeast; general: temperate eastern North America.

GERANIUM FAMILY
(Geraniaceae)

Wild Geranium
(Geranium maculatum)

Canada Tick Trefoil

Description Perennial with a clump of palmately divided basal leaves and a leafy stem, usually 1 to 3 feet tall, topped by conspicuous, pale rosy purple flowers. The flowers have 5 petals and are 1 to 2 inches across. When mature, the beaked seed pods split into 5 segments that suddenly coil upward, scattering the seeds. *Late spring, summer*

Habitat and Range Minnesota: throughout, except in the southwest and northeast; general: temperate eastern North America.

Comments Often grows on roadsides. Also called Crane's-bill. The cultivated geranium belongs to a different genus, *Pelargonium*, and comes from South Africa.

Related Species Bicknell's Geranium (*Geranium bicknellii*) is an annual or biennial with similar but smaller flowers, about ½ inch across. It grows mostly in the northern forest areas, especially on disturbed soils. Stems are spreading and sprawling.

Wild Geranium

Milkwort Family (*Polygalaceae*)

Fringed Polygala
(*Polygala paucifolia*)

Description A low perennial, usually 4 to 8 inches tall, of northern forests. The stem, which rises from a slender rootstock, has 3 to 6 oval leaves near the top and a few much smaller leaves below. The solitary rose or magenta flower is quite distinctive. It is of irregular shape and has a tufted fringe on the tip of the lower petal. *Spring, summer*

Fringed Polygala

Habitat and Range Minnesota: mostly in the north and east on sandy soil, where it often grows under pines; general: temperate eastern North America.

Comments Also called Bird-on-the-wing.

Evening Primrose Family (*Onagraceae*)

Fireweed (*Epilobium angustifolium*)

Description Clumped perennial of open and brushy uplands. It commonly grows 2 to 4 feet tall. The erect stems are usually reddish, have elongate alternate leaves, and end in a tapering cluster of rose purple flowers. Flowers have 4 petals and are 1 to 1½ inches across. The seeds, which are wind-borne by a tuft of hairs, are produced in slender pods that open from the top downward. *Summer*

Habitat and Range Minnesota: mostly in the east and north, often along roads; general: subarctic circumpolar, south to northern temperate United States.

Comments Fireweed rapidly invades sites of forest fires and often becomes the most conspicuous plant. Also called Great Willow Herb.

RICHARD HAUG

Fireweed

Scarlet Gaura (*Gaura coccinea*)

Description Prairie perennial with hairy, often branched stems, usually about a foot tall. The flowers have 4 pink to scarlet petals, are about ½ inch across, and are in an elongate inflorescence. *Summer*

Habitat and Range Minnesota: mostly along the western border; general: temperate central and western North America.

Comments Its name is from the Greek word for "showy."

BUCKWHEAT FAMILY
(*Polygonaceae*)

Swamp Smartweed
(*Polygonum coccineum*)

Scarlet Gaura

Description Perennial of marshes and shores, sometimes growing in shallow water. Usually it is 1 to 3 feet tall. It has small rosy flowers in elongate clusters and hairy alternate leaves. There is a tubular collar around the stem above the base of each leaf stalk. *Summer*

Habitat and Range Minnesota: widely distributed in wet, open places; general: temperate North America.

Related Species The Water Smartweed (*Polygonum amphibium*), also perennial, often grows in shallow water. Here it has floating leaves that are shiny green above and red beneath. The rosy flowers are in short, blunt clusters.

FOUR-O'CLOCK FAMILY
(*Nyctaginaceae*)

Wild Four-o'clock
(*Mirabilis nyctaginea*)

Description Erect perennial, usually 1 to 3 feet tall, with forking

Swamp Smartweed

Wild Four-o'clock

stems and stalked, heart-shaped leaves. The funnel-shaped rosy flowers rise from a saucerlike structure, the "umbrella." The flowers open in the afternoon and usually wilt by noon of the following day. Stems are markedly noded, tend to be 4-sided, and are hairless or nearly so. *Summer*

Habitat and Range Minnesota: throughout in dry, open places, often appearing uninvited in sunny dooryards and gardens; general: much of temperate North America.

Comments Also called Heart-leaved Umbrella-wort.

PURSLANE FAMILY (*Portulacaceae*)

Spring Beauty (*Claytonia virginica*)

Description A well-named spring wildflower of damp woods and clearings. The short stems, 6 to 10 inches tall, and the narrow, elongate leaves are both somewhat fleshy. Flowers are pink and in loose clusters. They have 5 petals that are veined with deeper pink. *Spring*

Habitat and Range Minnesota: in the east but most common in the southeast; general: eastern United States and adjacent Canada.

Related Species The Broad-leaved Spring Beauty (*Claytonia caroliniana*), which has wider and distinctly stalked leaves, is known in Minnesota in southern St. Louis County and north along the Lake Superior shore.

Spring Beauty

Bouncing Bet

PINK FAMILY (*Caryophyllaceae*)

Bouncing Bet
(*Saponaria officinalis*)

Description A European perennial that escaped from pioneer gardens to nearby roadsides. The showy clusters of pink flowers top leafy stems that are commonly 1 to 2 feet tall. Occasionally there are plants with semidouble flowers that range in color from white to rosy lilac. The plant, especially the rootstock, contains saponin, which produces slippery suds in water. *Late spring, summer*

Habitat and Range Widely naturalized in Minnesota and elsewhere in temperate North America.

Comments It was once used as a natural detergent for washing fine fabrics and is still used occasionally in museums for cleaning old tapestries. It makes a showy garden perennial but is aggressive and spreading.

HEATH FAMILY (*Ericaceae*)

Pink Shinleaf (*Pyrola asarifolia*)

Description The nodding flowers are pink or purple in an elongate, upright cluster. Leaves are basal. They are thick and shiny and have round or kidney-shaped blades. The plants often grow in patches. *Summer*

Habitat and Range Minnesota: mostly in the northern forested area, especially in the northeast; general: subarctic to temperate North America.

Swamp Laurel (*Kalmia polifolia*)

Description Low shrub of wet bogs and muskegs. Here it usually

Pink Shinleaf

grows with other small shrubs of the heath family. It has leathery opposite leaves and loose clusters of attractive rose pink flowers, each with 5 spreading petals united at the base. *Summer*

Habitat and Range Minnesota: forested areas of the north and center, most common in the northeast; general: subarctic North America south to northern United States.

Comments The leaves are poisonous to cattle and sheep but are tough and usually not eaten. *Kalmia* honors Peter Kalm (1715–79), Swedish botanist and early traveler in North America.

Bog Rosemary
(*Andromeda glaucophylla*)

Swamp Laurel

Description Low shrub, less than 2 feet tall, of wetter parts of bogs and muskegs. The alternate leaves are evergreen and narrow, and have rolled edges. The white or pinkish flowers are in small clusters on the upper part of the stem. They are urn-shaped with 5 united petals. *Summer*

Habitat and Range Minnesota: in the north and center, usually growing with other bog heaths; general: subarctic south to northern United States.

Comments In Greek mythology Andromeda was an Ethiopian princess who was chained to a rock by the sea and rescued from a sea monster by Perseus. The leaves, like those of *Kalmia* and probably *Ledum*, are poisonous to sheep.

Bog Cranberry
(*Vaccinium oxycoccus*)

Description A small cranberry growing, as

Bog Rosemary

its name suggests, in cool bogs, where it trails over the sphagnum. The small oval leaves are dark green with in-rolled margins. The undersides are whitish. The pale pink flowers with four backward-turning petals and a protruding clump of yellow stamens suggest tiny shooting stars hanging from the tips of small upright stalks. They are replaced in late summer by small red berries much like the cranberries of commerce in flavor and appearance but possibly more acidic. *Summer*

Habitat and Range Minnesota: boggy areas in north and east; general: northeastern United States. Circumboreal.

Comments Also called Small Cranberry.

Bog Cranberry

Lingonberry

WELBY SMITH

Lingonberry
(Vaccinium vitis-idaea)

Description Low, branched shrub, usually less than 6 inches tall, of mossy bogs and sometimes moist upland sites. The small leaves are elliptical, thick, and ever-green, and the flowers pink and bell-shaped. They are followed in late summer by red berries that are tart and much like cran-berries but have a distinctive flavor. *Summer*

Habitat and Range Minnesota: occasional in the north and northeast; general: widely distributed in arctic North America, including the east coast of Canada. Circumboreal.

Comments M. L. Fernald, noted botanist at Harvard, was of the opinion that lingonberries, not wild grapes, were the *vinber* from which the Vikings derived the name Vinland. Also called Mountain Cranberry.

DOGBANE FAMILY
(*Apocynaceae*)

Common Dogbane
(*Apocynum androsaemifolium*)

Description Bushy perennial, usually 1 to 2 feet tall, with spreading branches. A plant of roadsides, fields, and open woods, it has loose clusters of small pink to nearly white bell-shaped flowers. The elliptical leaves are opposite, and the plant contains milky juice. Seeds with a tuft of hair at one end are produced in paired pods. *Summer*

Habitat and Range Minnesota: throughout; general: widely distributed in North America.

Lingonberry (fruit)

EVELYN MOYLE

Comments Small flies are sometimes trapped in the blossoms when their proboscis is caught at the base of the anthers. Native Americans twisted the fibrous stem to make thread and bowstrings. This species has sometimes poisoned herbivorous animals. Dogbane is an ancient name, but we know of no dogs poisoned by it. Also called Spreading Dogbane.

Common Dogbane

Showy Milkweed

MILKWEED FAMILY
(*Asclepiadaceae*)

Showy Milkweed
(*Asclepias speciosa*)

Description Similar to the Common Milkweed, but the greenish purple flowers have longer and more tapering, upright petals (hoods) and an abundance of woolly hairs. *Summer*

Habitat and Range Minnesota: prairies in the west; general: temperate western North America.

Comments Stem fibers of this and some other milkweeds were used by Native Americans to make cords and rope.

Swamp Milkweed (*Asclepias incarnata*)

Description Common, erect perennial, usually 3 to 4 feet tall, of marshes and shores. It has clusters of pink to rose purple flowers, tapering opposite leaves, and milky juice. Often the entire plant is reddish. *Summer*

Habitat and Range Minnesota: throughout; general: temperate North America.

Comments This milkweed is quite ornamental and is sometimes grown in gardens. The root was used medicinally by the Ojibwe.

PHLOX FAMILY
(*Polemoniaceae*)

Downy Phlox
(*Phlox pilosa*)

Description Perennial of moist meadows, prairies, and open woods. Stems, which are often clumped, have opposite leaves

Swamp Milkweed

that are narrow and tapering. The flowers are pink or rosy, often with a darker center, or "eye." They are arranged in a spreading cluster. *Spring*

Habitat and Range Minnesota: throughout except in the northeast; general: a typical meadow and prairie plant throughout eastern temperate North America.

Comments Downy Phlox well exemplifies the name *phlox*, which is Greek for "flame." Also called Prairie Phlox and, by pioneers, Sweet William.

Downy Phlox

MINT FAMILY (*Lamiaceae*)

American Germander
(*Teucrium canadense*)

Description Upright, little-branched perennial of moist, often somewhat shady places. The hairy, square stems, usually 1 to 2 feet tall, bear stalked opposite leaves with blades that are rounded or tapering at the base. Flowers are 2-lipped, pink purple, and in spirelike clusters. The top of the corolla is split, making an opening through which the stamens protrude. *Summer*

Habitat and Range Minnesota: most common in southeastern third but occasionally in the north; general: temperate North America.

Comments Also called Wood Sage.

Common Woundwort
(*Stachys palustris*)

Description Upright, usually unbranched perennial of wet, open places. The stem, usually 1 to 2 feet tall, is square and hairy. The oppo-

American Germander

site leaves are stalkless or nearly so, with blades abruptly narrowed at the base. The rose purple flowers are in whorls on an elongate, tapering inflorescence. Each is 2-lipped, the upper lip covering the stamens. *Summer*

Habitat and Range Minnesota: throughout; general: subarctic and temperate North America.

Common Woundwort

Comments Woundwort was used by the Ojibwe as colic medicine. Also called Hedge Nettle.

Motherwort

Motherwort (*Leonurus cardiaca*)

Description Robust perennial, up to 4 feet tall, with square, erect, and usually clumped stems. The opposite leaves are lobed near the base, and the 2-lipped, pink flowers are in dense clusters in the leaf axils. The clustered sepals persist through the winter. In spring, growth starts as a clump of lobed basal leaves. *Summer*

Habitat and Range Minnesota: throughout in waste places, often in the dooryards and along paths; general: widely naturalized in North America.

Comments Motherwort is a native of eastern Asia and was originally cultivated as a medicinal herb.

False Dragonhead
(*Physostegia virginiana*)

Description Erect perennial, usually 2 to 3 feet tall, of marshes, moist open woods, and stream

banks. Stems and elongate opposite leaves are smooth and without hairs. The showy rosy pink flowers are about 1 inch long and in spirelike, often branched clusters. *Summer*

Habitat and Range Minnesota: throughout, but most common on river bottoms and in open floodplain forests in the east; general: eastern temperate North America.

Comments The plant is grown as a garden perennial. When the flower is pushed into a new position, it will remain there, giving the species the alternate name Obedient Plant, which is used in some seed catalogs.

FIGWORT FAMILY
(*Scrophulariaceae*)

False Dragonhead

Rough Gerardia
(*Agalinis aspera*)

Description A slender, branched annual of moist prairies, often growing among grasses. The bell-shaped rosy pink flowers are about 1 inch long and on ascending stalks. The stems and narrow leaves are rough with short hairs. *Summer*

Habitat and Range Minnesota: prairies in the west and south; general: temperate central North America.

Comments The common name commemorates John Gerarde (1545–1612), English botanist and herbalist. Also called False Foxglove.

Related Species The Small-flowered Gerardia (*Agalinis paupercula*) has similar but smaller flowers and smooth leaves and stems. It grows in damp meadows, marshes, and seepage areas.

Rough Gerardia

137

Indian Paintbrush
(*Castilleja coccinea*)

Description Among the brightest of summer wildflowers. It is an annual with erect stems, usually 1 to 2 feet tall. The stem is topped with a cluster of bright red or, less commonly, yellow leaves, which might be mistaken for petals. Among these colored leaves are the inconspicuous, 2-lipped yellowish flowers. The green stem leaves have narrow, pointed lobes. *Summer*

Habitat and Range Minnesota: throughout, except in the southwest and extreme west; general: temperate eastern North America.

Comments Indian Paintbrush is semiparasitic, its roots tapping those of other plants. Also called Painted Cup.

Indian Paintbrush

Related Species The rarer Downy Painted Cup (*Castilleja sessiliflora*) is a prairie plant, usually less than 1 foot tall. Its leaves are covered with soft gray hairs.

Twin Flower

HONEYSUCKLE FAMILY
(*Caprifoliaceae*)

Twin Flower
(*Linnaea borealis*)

Description Low, trailing perennial of cool, moist woods and bogs. The nodding pink flowers are bell-shaped, about ½ inch long, and in pairs at the top of slender stalks. Leaves are evergreen and opposite on the stems. *Summer*

Habitat and Range Minnesota: northern

and east-central parts, mostly in coniferous forests and muskegs; general: circumpolar, from subarctic south to temperate regions.

Comments *Linnaea* commemorates Carl Linnaeus (1707–78), the father of modern plant classification. This plant was his favorite wildflower.

Bellflower Family (*Campanulaceae*)

Cardinal Flower (*Lobelia cardinalis*)

Description Perennial of damp, open or somewhat shady places. Commonly 2 to 3 feet tall. The intense red flowers are in an elongate cluster. Each is about 1 inch across and has 3 spreading lower petals and 2 upright petals. The petals are united into a tube toward their base. Occasionally plants have white or rose flowers. Juice is milky and acrid. *Summer*

Habitat and Range Minnesota: mostly in the east as far north as Pine County, especially along streams; general: temperate eastern North America.

RICHARD HAUG

Cardinal Flower

Comments Cardinal Flower has long been grown in gardens. It requires a moist spot and will tolerate some shade.

Lily Family (*Liliaceae*)

Prairie Onion (*Allium stellatum*)

Description Has slender, solid leaves and stems, and erect umbels of small pink or rosy flowers. The bulb has papery scales. *Spring, summer*

Habitat and Range Minnesota: prairies and meadows throughout but most common in the south and west; general: central North America.

Related Species Wild Leek (*Allium tricoccum*), also called ramp, an onion of hardwood forests, has long, flat leaves that are shiny and pointed. They have a strong garlic odor and may be used in salads—with discretion. In summer, after the leaves are gone, an umbel of whitish flowers is produced.

Prairie Onion

Minnesota Trout Lily
(*Erythronium propullans*)

Description Low perennial of moist woods, especially river bottoms and ravines. Leaves are similar but smaller than those of the White Trout Lily. The flower is pale pink and about ½ inch across. *Spring*

Habitat and Range Minnesota: known only from a few locations in Rice, Goodhue, and Steele Counties and nowhere else in the world.

Comments This rare wildflower was described in 1871 from a specimen collected by Mary B. Hedges, teacher of botany at Faribault. She sent it to botanist Asa Gray at Harvard, who gave it its botanical name. Some plants have been transplanted to the University of Minnesota Arboretum at Chanhassen, where they may be seen in bloom in spring.

Minnesota Trout Lily

ORCHID FAMILY
(*Orchidaceae*)

Stemless Lady's-slipper
(*Cypripedium acaule*)

Description Perennial with 2 oval basal leaves and a flower stalk usually 6 to 8 inches tall. It is topped by a showy rose purple flower. The lip, or "slipper," is about 2 inches long and cleft or split above. *Spring, early summer*

Habitat and Range Minnesota: mostly in the north on acid soils

Stemless Lady's-slipper

Showy Lady's-slipper

(pH 4 to 5) of bogs, swamps, and coniferous forests; general: eastern United States and adjacent Canada.

Comments As in other lady's-slippers, the flower is marvelously modified as an insect trap. Insects that enter the lip can escape only by going upward past the modified stamens and pistil, thereby pollinating the flowers. Also called Moccasin Flower.

Showy Lady's-slipper
(Cypripedium reginae)

Description Large lady's-slipper with leafy stems, 2 to 3 feet tall. They end in 1 or 2 showy flowers. The rounded, inflated lip is 1 to 1½ inches long and is white, marked with pink or rosy purple. Hairs on the leaves and stem sometimes cause a skin rash. *Late spring, summer*

Habitat and Range Minnesota: swamps and moist woods in the north and east on limy, neutral soils; general: eastern United States and adjacent Canada.

Comments Showy Lady's-slipper is Minnesota's state flower. The plants are long-lived and slow to develop, requiring about 15 years from seed germination to flowering. Also called Pink-and-White Lady's-slipper.

Showy Orchis
(Galearis spectabilis)

Description Low perennial of hardwood forests. Usually 6 to 8 inches tall. It has 2 rather thick basal leaves and several small spurred flowers in an elongate cluster. The lip is white. Other petals and the sepals are pink or purplish and unite to form a hood. *Late spring*

Showy Orchis

Habitat and Range Minnesota: mostly in the southeastern third, including the Twin Cities area, but not rare; general: eastern temperate North America.

Comments If a pin is inserted into the spur of the flower, tiny club-shaped pollen masses will adhere to it. Such pollen masses (pollinia) are transported on the mouth parts of insects to the pistils of other flowers. Pollinated by bumblebees and probably by other nectar feeders.

Dragon's Mouth (*Arethusa bulbosa*)

Description A conspicuous and beautiful bog orchid. The stem, usually 6 to 8 inches tall, has a single leaf and ends in an odd-shaped flower about 1¼ inches across. The lip is pale pink dotted with yellow and purple. The ascending petals and sepals are a deeper pink. Pollinated by bumblebees. *Early summer*

Habitat and Range Minnesota: rare, in bogs and grassy swamps, mostly in the northeast; general: temperate eastern North America.

Related Species Two other conspicuous rosy or pink orchids with flowers about the same size grow in Minnesota bogs. The Snake Mouth (*Pogonia ophioglossoides*) has a solitary flower much like that of Dragon's Mouth but with a fringed lip. Grass Pink (*Calopogon tuberosus*) has a cluster of several pink flowers with spreading petals and sepals. The lip is at the top of the flower, in this respect differing from most other orchids.

Dragon's Mouth

Calypso (*Calypso bulbosa*)

Description Among the rarest and most beautiful of northern orchids. In early spring the short, flowering stalk, usually 2 to 5 inches tall, rises from the base of a broad leaf that has survived the winter. The flower has a slipper-shaped lip that is white marked with yellow, purple, and brown. Behind it are 5 narrow purple or rose petals and sepals, often standing erect much like the feathers on an Indian bonnet. *Early spring*

Habitat and Range Minnesota: rare, in coniferous forests, woods, and swamps of the north; general: circumpolar, in North America south to northern United States and in mountains to Arizona.

Calypso

Comments Calypso was the nymph whose charms delayed Ulysses for seven years on his journey home from Troy.

Spotted Coral Root
(Corallorhiza maculata)

Description A saprophytic orchid that lives in partnership with a soil fungus and has no chlorophyll. The pinkish purple stems, mostly less than 1 foot tall, rise from a mass of coral-like roots. Leaves are reduced to sheaths, and the small flowers are in an elongate cluster. Petals and lip are white, usually tinted and spotted with purple. *Late spring, summer*

Habitat and Range Minnesota: moist woods in north and east; general: much of temperate North America.

Comments Other orchids also live in partnership with a fungus but do not carry this relationship as far as do the coral roots.

Related Species The Striped Coral Root (*Corallorhiza striata*) has reddish purple stems and purplish flowers with striped petals. It grows in moist woods.

PITCHER PLANT FAMILY
(Sarraceniaceae)

Pitcher Plant
(Sarracenia purpurea)

Description Insectivorous plant of bogs and wet sedgy swamps. It has a rosette of pitcher-shaped leaves. These partly fill with water. Insects find descent into the pitcher easy, but downward-pointing hairs hinder climbing out. Drowned insects

Spotted Coral Root

Pitcher Plant

are broken down by enzymes and bacteria, and provide nutrients for the plant. The dark red flowers, about 2 inches across, are nodding and single on leafless stems. *Summer*

Habitat and Range Minnesota: mostly in the north; general: subarctic North America south to southeastern United States.

Blue *to* Purple
FLOWERS

CROWFOOT FAMILY
(*Ranunculaceae*)

Pasque Flower
(*Anemone patens*)

Description Early spring perennial of prairies. The flower is about 2 inches across and has 5 to 7 pale purple sepals. It tops a hairy stem on which is a cluster (whorl) of divided, protective leaves. Usually there are several flowering stems in a clump. Within the flower is a ring of golden stamens and a central tuft of grayish pistils that become plumed fruits. In summer there is a clump of divided basal leaves. *Early spring*

Pasque Flower

Habitat and Range Minnesota: dry prairies and open hillsides in the south and west; general: much of western North America. Also in Eurasia.

Comments Pasque Flower often blooms during the Easter (Paschal) season. To prairie children, the hairy plants with bent flower buds were "Goslings." It is the floral emblem of South Dakota and Manitoba. The plant is unpalatable to grazing animals. Also called Crocus.

Wild Lupine

BEAN FAMILY (*Fabaceae*)

Wild Lupine (*Lupinus perennis*)

Description A handsome wild perennial with elongate, spikelike clusters of blue flowers. It usually grows on sandy soil and is 1 to 3 feet tall. The leaves are palmately compound with 7 to 11 leaflets. The fruit is a hairy pod. *Late spring, summer*

Habitat and Range Minnesota: sandy prairies and savannas in the center and southeast; general: eastern United States.

Comments Its name is derived from *lupus*, the Latin word for "wolf," and is based on the ancient but mistaken assumption that since Lupine grows on poor soils, it is responsible for this condition.

Silver-leaved Psoralea
(Pediomelum argophyllum)

Description A common prairie perennial with leaves and stems covered with soft white hairs. Stems are branched, somewhat zigzag, and usually 1 to 2 feet tall. Leaves are palmately compound with 3 or 5 leaflets. It has small blue flowers. *Summer*

Habitat and Range Minnesota: dry prairies, mostly in the south and west; general: prairies and plains of upper central and western United States and adjacent Canada.

Comments Also called Scurf Pea.

Silver-leaved Psoralea

Prairie Turnip *(Pediomelum esculentum)*

Description This perennial plant, which grows to a height of 18 inches, has an upright, hairy stem and palmately compound leaves with 5 elongate leaflets. The small blue flowers are in a dense, oblong cluster. *Summer*

Habitat and Range Minnesota: in the south and west on prairies, often where hilly; general: prairies and plains, north-central and western United States and adjacent Canada.

Comments An important food plant of Native Americans of the Great Plains, who dug the thick, turniplike root to obtain the central starchy portion. The Dakota called it Teepsenee, and early French explorers of Minnesota named the Pomme de Terre River after it. Also called Pomme Blanche and Indian Potato.

Prairie Turnip

147

Lead Plant

Lead Plant (*Amorpha canescens*)

Description Perennial of prairies. The erect, somewhat woody stems are usually 1 to 2 feet tall. They are tipped by tapering spikes of small blue flowers, each having a single petal that is shorter than the golden yellow stamens. Leaves are pinnately compound with many leaflets. They are gray with soft hairs, giving the plant both its leaden hue and its name. *Summer*

Habitat and Range Minnesota: prairies; general: temperate western North America.

Comments Because its tough rootstocks hindered plowing, pioneer prairie farmers called it "Devil's Shoestrings." To Ponca Indians, it was "Buffalo-bellow Plant" because it blossomed when bison were in rut.

Purple Prairie Clover (*Dalea purpurea*)

Description A common perennial of dry prairies. Elongate heads of purple flowers top slender, erect stems, usually about 2 feet tall. Leaves are pinnately compound with narrow leaflets that are dotted beneath. It often grows in patches. *Summer*

Habitat and Range Minnesota: dry prairies and open places but uncommon in the northeast; general: temperate central and western North America.

Related Species The White Prairie Clover (*Dalea candida*) is similar in appearance and distribution but has white flowers and is usually somewhat taller than Purple Prairie Clover.

Purple Prairie Clover

Locoweed (*Oxytropis lambertii*)

Description A low prairie perennial, usually less than 8 inches tall. It has a basal clump of pinnately compound leaves that tend to stand upright. They are covered with silky hairs. Flowers are reddish purple and in an elongate cluster on a leafless stalk. The keel of the flower has a point at the front end (tip), in this respect differing from several, more western locoweeds of the genus *Astragalus*. Summer

Habitat and Range Minnesota: dry prairies, mostly in the west, but uncommon. It was once common on the hills along the upper Minnesota River; general: Great Plains.

Locoweed

Comments Locoweed has long been known to be poisonous to stock. Animals become addicted to it, lose muscular coordination, and become lethargic: "go loco."

Prairie Plum (*Astragalus crassicarpus*)

Description Low, clumped perennial, usually with several spreading stems and seldom taller than 1 foot. It has pinnately compound leaves with many small leaflets and rounded clusters of purple or sometimes whitish flowers about 1 inch long. The thick-walled, inflated pods commonly lie on the ground. They are shaped like small plums and when young, have a texture and flavor much like garden peas. *Spring*

Habitat and Range Minnesota: dry prairies in the south and west, often on hills and bluffs; general: prairies and plains of western United States and adjacent Canada.

Prairie Plum

Prairie Plum (fruit)

American Vetch
(*Vicia americana*)

Description A widely distributed perennial herb of grassy and brushy places, commonly 2 to 3 feet long with alternate compound leaves. It has purple flowers in clusters of 2 to 9. The paired stipules (leaflike structures at the base of the compound leaves) are sharply toothed. The only native vetch in Minnesota. *Spring, summer*

Habitat and Range Minnesota: throughout in grassy habitats and brushy places; general: temperate North America.

American Vetch

Related Species Tufted Vetch (*Vicia cracca*) has 1-sided clusters of many (9 to 30) blue or purple flowers and pinnately compound leaves ending in a tendril. Hairs on the stem lie flat and are inconspicuous. The Hairy Vetch (*Vicia villosa*), annual or biennial, is similar but has soft, spreading hairs. Both species are of European origin but are widely naturalized in Minnesota and elsewhere in North America.

Purple Pea

Purple Pea (*Lathyrus venosus*)

Description A perennial vine rising from a rootstock. Flowers are purple or bicolored purple and white and in an elongate cluster of 10 or more. Leaves are compound, end in a tendril, and have stipules (paired leaflike structures at the base of the leafstalk) that are smaller than the leaflets. *Spring, summer*

Habitat and Range Minnesota: throughout in woods and brushy places and on prairies; general: temperate North America.

Related Species The Pale Vetchling (*Lathyrus ochroleucus*), also called White Pea, a perennial, has yellowish white flowers, pale foliage, and stipules larger than the side leaflets. It occurs mostly in woods and brushy places.

Beach Pea (*Lathyrus japonicus*)

Description Perennial, quite similar to the Purple Pea but usually lower growing and with stipules larger than the side leaflets. *Summer*

Habitat and Range Circumpolar on beaches of oceans and large northern lakes. In Minnesota it is common on beaches of Lake Superior.

Comments It is doubtful that the seeds of this and other wild peas are edible, although in Europe, Beach Pea has been used for food in times of famine.

Related Species The Marsh Pea (*Lathyrus palustris*), a climbing perennial, grows in marshes and along shores. It has purple flowers, leaves with stipules much smaller than the narrow leaflets, and often winged (flanged) stems. It is found throughout much of Minnesota.

Beach Pea

Hog Peanut (*Amphicarpea bracteata*)

Description Annual slender, twining vine of moist woods, thickets, and banks. Leaves are compound with 3 broad leaflets. On the upper part of the vine are small white to lavender flowers in loose clusters. Near the base are other flowers that are nearly or entirely without petals. They are directed downward and produce rounded 1-seeded pods, often underground. These are the "hog peanuts." *Summer*

Habitat and Range Minnesota: throughout, uncommon in the southwest; general: eastern temperate North America.

RICHARD HAUG

Hog Peanut

Wood Sorrel Family
(*Oxalidaceae*)

Violet Wood Sorrel
(*Oxalis violacea*)

Description Low perennial, a few inches tall, with a clump of basal leaves. The small leaf is compound with 3 leaflets, each notched at the end. Flowers are violet and in a small cluster at the end of the stalk. They have 5 spreading petals. *Spring, summer*

Habitat and Range Minnesota: woods and prairies, mostly in the south; general: eastern United States.

Violet Wood Sorrel

Comments Leaves of this and the yellow species of *Oxalis* contain oxalic acid and have a sour taste. Both *sorrel* and *oxalis* mean "sour." Children often call the plant sauerkraut or Sour Grass.

Violet Family (*Violaceae*)

Hooked Violet
(*Viola adunca*)

Description A woodland violet, often of open pine forests. It has small blue flowers, leaves usually less than 1 inch wide, and leafy stems covered with minute hairs. These hairs are visible under a hand lens. Stems are first erect and clumped but later trail to form patches. *Spring, summer*

Hooked Violet

Habitat and Range
Minnesota: mostly in the north; general: temperate North America.

Related Species The Dog Violet (*Viola conspersa*) has similar growth habits. However, the leafy stems are hairless, or nearly so, and the flowers range from pale blue to nearly white. It grows in moist places.

Prairie Violet
(Viola pedatifida)

Description A fairly common prairie violet. Its petals are all the same shade of blue, and the lower petals are bearded on the inside near the base. Leaves are divided. *Spring*

Habitat and Range Minnesota: meadows and prairies of western and southern Minnesota; general: temperate North America.

RICHARD HAUG

Prairie Violet

Comments Also called Bearded Bird's-foot Violet.

Related Species Pansy Violet or Bird's-foot Violet (*Viola pedata*) is characterized by deeply lobed leaves and flowers that are flat-faced and often 1 inch across. The upper petals are deeper blue than the lower, and all of the petals are hairless. Found mostly in southeastern Minnesota.

Downy Blue Violet *(Viola sororia)*

Description Commonest of blue violets with hairy basal leaves and no leafy stems. The leaf blades are toothed and about as long as wide. The leaves usually overtop the flowers. *Spring*

Habitat and Range Minnesota: throughout in moist meadows and open woods; general: eastern temperate North America.

Comments Also called Woolly Blue Violet.

Related Species The New England Violet (*Viola novae-angliae*) also has blue flowers and hairy basal leaves, but the leaf blades are markedly longer than wide. It is a plant of coarse soils and rocky places, especially along streams. In Minnesota it grows mostly in the north.

Downy Blue Violet

Purple Loosestrife

Loosestrife Family (*Lythraceae*)

Purple Loosestrife (*Lythrum salicaria*)

Description Stout perennial of marshes and shores. It is often 3 to 4 feet tall with conspicuous elongate clusters of rosy purple flowers. The flower has 6 crinkled petals. Leaves are opposite or whorled. *Summer*

Habitat and Range Minnesota: naturalized in marshes and along streams in the Twin Cities area and less commonly elsewhere; general: a Eurasian species long established in eastern North America.

Comments Purple Loosestrife became conspicuous in Minnesota about 1940 and has continued to spread westward. It grows in patches, produces many seeds, and has few or no natural enemies. It takes over wetlands and displaces native species and is listed as a noxious weed in Minnesota, where state law requires that it be destroyed wherever found. Also called Spiked Loosestrife.

Gentian Family (*Gentianaceae*)

Closed Gentian (*Gentiana andrewsii*)

Description Perennial, usually 1 to 2 feet tall, with upright stems that end in clusters of club- or bottle-shaped blue flowers. The top of the flower is closed or nearly so, making the interior available only to large insects, such as bumblebees, that can push the petals apart. The toothless leaves are opposite with a pair of nerves in addition to the midrib. *Autumn*

Closed Gentian

Habitat and Range Minnesota: throughout, in moist, undisturbed open or somewhat shaded areas; general: temperate eastern North America.

Comments Also called Bottle Gentian.

Downy Gentian

Downy Gentian
(Gentiana puberulenta)

Description Perennial of dry prairies and open woods. The stems, usually 6 to 12 inches long and often somewhat sprawling, end in 1 or more dark blue or blue purple flowers. Each has 5 petals that are spreading above but joined below to form a tube. *Autumn*

Habitat and Range Minnesota: on prairies in the south and west; general: temperate central North America.

Comments The name *gentian* harks back to Gentius, king of ancient Illyria, who is said to have discovered the medicinal value of gentian root.

Fringed Gentian
(Gentianopsis crinita)

Description Perhaps the most beautiful of autumn wildflowers. This biennial prefers moist, limy sites, such as calcareous fens, shores, and seepage areas. The plant, usually 8 to 24 inches tall, is often branched above and has opposite leaves. It has conspicuous blue flowers with 4 spreading petals that are fringed at the end and part way down the sides. The petals are twisted together when the flower is closed. *Autumn*

Habitat and Range Minnesota: mostly in the east and north, but local; general: temperate eastern North America.

Fringed Gentian

MILKWEED FAMILY
(*Asclepiadaceae*)

Common Milkweed
(*Asclepias syriaca*)

Description Robust perennial of open places. It is often 3 to 4 feet tall and grows in patches. The erect, hairy stems have elliptical opposite leaves and stalked clusters of greenish purple flowers. The upright petals are hoodlike and rounder and shorter than the sepals below them. The juice is milky. The flat seeds are wind-borne by a tuft of silky hairs. *Summer*

Habitat and Range Minnesota: throughout, but uncommon in the northeast; general: temperate eastern North America.

Comments Stems with open pods, from which the seeds have been released, are gathered for winter bouquets. Young stems, pods, and flower buds have sometimes been cooked and eaten like asparagus. The flowers are rich in nectar and attract many insects.

Common Milkweed

PHLOX FAMILY (*Polemoniaceae*)

Wild Blue Phlox
(*Phlox divaricata*)

Description A perennial of rich woods. The stems, usually about 1 foot tall, rise from slender root-stocks. When in bloom, the plants form pale blue clumps and patches. Occasionally plants have white or purplish flowers. They are in flat-topped clusters and are faintly fragrant. The flower has 5 spreading petals that are united below to form a tube. *Spring*

Common Milkweed (fruit)

Habitat and Range Minnesota: most common in the southeastern third; general: eastern temperate North America.

Comments Wild Blue Phlox does well in a shady garden spot if given good soil and plenty of moisture. Also called Wood Phlox.

Wild Blue Phlox

Jacob's Ladder
(Polemonium reptans)

Description A perennial, 6 to 18 inches high, with deep blue bell-shaped flowers ½ to ¾ inch across, hanging at the ends of weak, branched stems. The leaves have paired, slender leaflets that make up the "ladder" of its common name. *Summer*

Habitat and Range Minnesota: most abundant in southeast corner but grows in rich woods and bottomlands as far north as Mille Lacs; general: northeastern United States south to North Carolina.

Comments It may be grown in gardens in rich, moist soil, preferably with other low-growing plants. Also called Greek Valerian.

WATERLEAF FAMILY
(Hydrophyllaceae)

Virginia Waterleaf
(Hydrophyllum virginianum)

Description Common perennial of upland woods and shady floodplains. It grows 1 to 2 feet tall and spreads by rootstocks. The large basal and stem leaves are deeply divided into irregularly toothed and sometimes lobed segments. Often the leaves have white splotches on them. These were once thought to contain water,

Jacob's Ladder

Virginia Waterleaf

hence the name. The white to pale purple bell-shaped flowers are in dense clusters, each flower having 5 protruding stamens, which give the clusters a fringed appearance. *Spring*

Habitat and Range Minnesota: throughout, except in extreme northeast; general: temperate eastern North America.

Comments Early spring leaves may be cooked and eaten like spinach.

BORAGE FAMILY (*Boraginaceae*)

Forget-me-not
(*Myosotis scorpioides*)

Description This European plant sometimes escapes from cultivation and becomes naturalized along streams and in seepage areas. It tolerates some shade and can grow in shallow water. The bright blue flowers are ¼ to ½ inch across. It is perennial with creeping, rooting stems from which rise short, erect flowering stalks. *Spring*

Habitat and Range Minnesota: in the east, common along Minnehaha Creek below the falls; general: throughout temperate North America.

Related Species The Bay Forget-me-not (*Myosotis laxa*) is similar but with smaller flowers, and usually it is not creeping. It is known from moist places in north-central Minnesota.

Forget-me-not

Virginia Bluebell
(*Mertensia virginica*)

Description A perennial, mostly 1 to 2 feet tall, with leafy, often clumped stems. The nodding blue flowers, about 1 inch long, are in a loose cluster. Buds are pink. The blunt, hairless leaves are without teeth and have a bluish cast. *Spring*

Virginia Bluebell

Habitat and Range Minnesota: moist woods and river bottoms in the southeast; general: eastern United States south to Alabama. It is often planted in gardens and blossoms along with daffodils.

Comments Also called Virginia Cowslip.

Related Species The Tall Lungwort (*Mertensia paniculata*), locally called Bluebell, has similar blue flowers, but the leaves are pointed and hairy on both sides. In Minnesota it is found mostly in the northeast, especially along Lake Superior. It is a northern and western species.

VERVAIN FAMILY (*Verbenaceae*)

Blue Vervain (*Verbena hastata*)

Description Robust, usually clumped perennial of roadsides, pastures, and drier marshes. Stems, generally 2 to 4 feet tall, are square with tapering opposite leaves that are coarsely toothed and often lobed. The small deep blue flowers are in slender spikes, several of which top the individual stems. Occasionally the flowers are pink. *Summer*

Habitat and Range Minnesota: throughout; general: eastern United States and adjacent Canada.

Comments Both the common and botanical names mean "sacred

Blue Vervain

bough," referring to ceremonial uses of a related species by Greeks and Romans.

Hoary Vervain (*Verbena stricta*)

Description Erect, square-stemmed perennial, usually 1 to 3 feet tall, of pastures, roadsides, and open places. Leaves are oval, coarsely toothed, and covered with soft hairs. The flowers are usually mauve purple but sometimes rose or blue. They are in a cluster of elongate spikes at the top of the stem. *Summer*

Habitat and Range Minnesota: mostly in the south and west; general: widely distributed in interior North America.

Related Species White Vervain (*Verbena urticifolia*) is a coarse, erect herb with tiny white flowers on long, slender spikes. It grows in fields and waste places, sometimes near buildings and in shady places.

Hoary Vervain

Common Skullcap

MINT FAMILY (*Lamiaceae*)

Common Skullcap
(*Scutellaria galericulata*)

Description Slender perennial, usually 1 to 2 feet tall, of marshes, bogs, and shores. Stems are square, and leaves are opposite. The 2-lipped blue flowers, about 1 inch long, are in the axils of the upper leaves. The calyx has a ridge or crest. *Summer*

Habitat and Range Minnesota: throughout; general: much of subarctic and temperate North America.

Related Species Flowers of the Mad-dog Skullcap (*Scutellaria* *lateriflora*) are smaller and in loose clusters in the axils of the oval, pointed leaves. It is a common plant of moist places and once had a considerable but unwarranted reputation for treatment of hydrophobia.

Fragrant Giant Hyssop
(*Agastache foeniculum*)

Description One of the most ornamental of our native mints. It is perennial, commonly 2 to 4 feet tall, with dense, often interrupted spikes of bright blue flowers. The leaves are toothed, opposite, and white beneath and have an anise or licorice odor when crushed. *Summer*

Habitat and Range Minnesota: throughout in dry, open or semi-shady places, and often along roads; general: central and western North America.

Fragrant Giant Hyssop

Ground Ivy
(*Glechoma hederacea*)

Description Low, strongly scented perennial with slender, creeping stems. They are square and root at the nodes. In spring short, leafy, upright stems are produced on which are 2-lipped blue flowers. Leaves are opposite and have wide, coarsely toothed blades. *Spring, summer*

Habitat and Range Minnesota: throughout in shady places, especially where the soil has been disturbed. Carpets the floodplains of many southeastern streams; general: a Eurasian species widely naturalized in North America.

Comments Also called Creeping Charlie.

Ground Ivy

Heal-all

Heal-all *(Prunella vulgaris)*

Description Perennial, usually less than 1 foot tall, of moist, open, semishady places. Often grows in patches. Leaves are opposite, and the stem is square. The purple blue flowers are in a short, thick spike, which also contains broad, pointed green or purplish bracts. *Spring, summer*

Habitat and Range Minnesota: widely distributed in moist, often shady places; general: subarctic to temperate North America. Also in Eurasia.

Comments Heal-all, as its name implies, was once used in folk medicine. The herbage is bitter and has little odor. Also called All-heal and Self-heal.

Wild Bergamot
(Monarda fistulosa)

Description Clumped perennial, usually 1 to 2 feet tall, growing in dry, open or brushy places. Often common on roadsides. The erect, square stems and opposite leaves are usually hairy. The lavender or pink flowers have 2 lips and are arranged in heads. Leaves and stems have a strong odor. *Summer*

Habitat and Range Minnesota: mostly in the south and west, where it is a conspicuous summer wildflower on dry prairies; general: temperate North America.

Comments Native Americans used this and related species to treat digestive and respiratory ailments. The odor of the leaves combines mint and citrus. Bergamot is a kind of orange. Also called Horsemint.

Wild Bergamot

Bittersweet Nightshade

NIGHTSHADE FAMILY (*Solanaceae*)

Bittersweet Nightshade
(*Solanum dulcamara*)

Description
Sprawling or climbing perennial vine. The clustered flowers have backward-curved petals and a central yellow "beak" of stamens and the pistil. The bright red berries are eaten by birds but are doubtfully edible for humans. *Summer*

Habitat and Range Minnesota: throughout in moist, brushy places; general: a Eurasian native now widely naturalized in North America.

Comments The berries contain an alkaloid, dulcamarin, which has had medicinal uses. The leaves, which may be lobed, have a sweet and then a bitter taste, hence the name. Also called Bittersweet and Poison Nightshade.

FIGWORT FAMILY (*Scrophulariaceae*)

Square-stemmed Monkey-flower (*Mimulus ringens*)

Description Erect perennial, usually 1 to 2 feet tall, of wet, open or brushy places. The 4-sided, bluntly angled stem bears toothed opposite leaves. In the axils of the leaves are the conspicuous blue flowers. They are stalked, 2-lipped, and about 1 inch long. *Summer*

Habitat and Range Minnesota: throughout; general: temperate eastern North America.

Comments *Mimulus* is Latin for "little buffoon" and refers to the "grin" that can be produced by squeezing the sides of the corolla.

Related Species The Yellow Monkey-flower (*Mimulus glabratus*) is a low, spreading plant of spring seepage areas and edges of streams. It

RICHARD HAUG

Square-stemmed Monkey-flower

163

often grows in shallow water. The flowers are like those of Square-stemmed Monkey-flower but are pale yellow and about ½ inch long.

Large-flowered Penstemon
(*Penstemon grandiflorus*)

Description One of the most beautiful of prairie wildflowers. The pale purple bell-shaped flowers, about 2 inches long, are in an elongate, spikelike cluster. The plant is perennial, usually 2 to 3 feet tall, and the bluish green stem leaves are opposite, rather wide, and without teeth. *Summer*

Habitat and Range Minnesota: sandy prairies in center and west; general: central United States.

Comments This and other penstemons are often called Beard-tongue because 1 of the 5 stamens has no anther and is hairy.

Large-flowered Penstemon

Related Species The Slender Penstemon (*Penstemon gracilis*) has smaller pale purple flowers, about ¾ inch long, is lower growing, and has narrow, toothed leaves. It is found in grassy places throughout much of Minnesota.

Harebell

EVELYN MOYLE

BELLFLOWER FAMILY
(*Campanulaceae*)

Harebell (*Campanula rotundifolia*)

Description Graceful and common perennial of dry prairies, roadsides, open woods, and rocky places. The clumped, slender stems range in height from a few inches to more than 1 foot. Stem leaves are elongate and pointed, and the bell-shaped blue flowers are in a loose cluster. Basal leaves are rounded or bluntly heart-shaped, hence the specific name. As in other members of this genus, the juice is milky. *Summer*

Habitat and Range Minnesota: throughout, except in the extreme south and southwest; general: Arctic circumpolar, south in North America to temperate United States.

Comments Harebell is easily cultured in gardens and does well in rockeries. Also called Bluebell and Bluebells of Scotland.

European Bellflower
(*Campanula rapunculoides*)

Description Perennial of roadsides and waste places, often near old gardens and dooryards. It has stiff, erect stems, 1 to 3 feet tall, ending in elongate, 1-sided clusters of pale purple bell-shaped flowers. They are nodding and about 1 inch long. The plants spread by rootstocks and often form patches. *Summer*

European Bellflower

Habitat and Range A European plant once grown in gardens and now widely naturalized in Minnesota and elsewhere in North America.

Related Species The Clustered Bellflower (*Campanula glomerata*), also from Europe, is well established along roads near Duluth. It is an erect perennial, usually 1 to 2 feet tall, with the stem ending in a compact cluster of bluish purple flowers.

American Bellflower
(*Campanula americana*)

Description Erect annual or biennial, usually 2 to 4 feet tall. The blue flowers are in a leafy spike.

American Bellflower

Great Blue Lobelia

Each flower is about 1 inch wide with 5 spreading petals joined at the base. There is a long, curved style in the center. Leaves are toothed and taper toward both ends. *Summer*

Habitat and Range Minnesota: mostly in the southern one-third in moist woods and along shady streams; general: temperate eastern North America.

Comments Also called Tall Bellflower.

Great Blue Lobelia
(Lobelia siphilitica)

Description Erect perennial, usually 1 to 2 feet tall, of wet places. The flowers resemble those of the Cardinal Flower but are blue or occasionally white. *Summer, autumn*

Habitat and Range Minnesota: throughout, often in swamps and along streams and ditches; general: temperate eastern North America.

Comments This species has sometimes been called Hi-belia to contrast it, perhaps facetiously, with lower-growing, blue-flowered kinds. It and several other members of the genus contain a toxic compound, lobeline. *Lobelia* honors Matthias de l'Obel (1538–1616), a Flemish botanist.

Pale-spike Lobelia
(Lobelia spicata)

Description A slender, single-stemmed plant, usually 1 to 2 feet tall, with small uniformly blue flowers on short stalks with a long inflorescence. *Summer*

Pale-spike Lobelia

Habitat and Range Minnesota: throughout but primarily in dry prairies and meadows in the south and west; general: subarctic North America south to northern United States.

Related Species Kalm's Lobelia (*Lobelia kalmii*) is a beautiful low-growing lobelia, usually less than 1 foot tall. The small pale blue flowers are about ½ inch across, have white centers, and are each on a slender stalk. Also called Northern Lobelia.

ASTER FAMILY (*Asteraceae*)

Purple Coneflower
(*Echinacea angustifolia*)

Purple Coneflower

Description A perennial, usually 2 to 3 feet tall, of dry prairies. Flower heads have purple rays and a raised, spiny center. The slender stem and 3-nerved leaves are covered with coarse hairs. *Summer*

Habitat and Range Minnesota: prairies, mostly in the west; general: temperate western North America.

Comments According to Lycurgus Moyer, pioneer Minnesota jurist and botanist, early travelers on the prairie called it Thirst Plant because the roots had a "salty, peppery taste." When they were chewed, the flow of saliva was increased, relieving the traveler's thirst when good drinking water was not to be had.

Large-leaved Aster
(*Aster macrophyllus*)

Description A common plant of northern forests, the heart-shaped basal leaves often covering the

EVELYN MOYLE

Large-leaved Aster

forest floor. Leaves are coarsely toothed and rough to touch. The flowering stems, mostly 1 to 2 feet tall, are topped by a spreading cluster of flower heads, each with 9 to 20 pale purple rays. *Autumn*

Habitat and Range Minnesota: upland forests, especially in the north; general: temperate eastern North America.

Lindley's Aster

Comments This and Lindley's Aster are perennials blooming in late summer and autumn. The flower heads have narrow rays that are white, blue, or purple. Stem leaves are alternate, and the crushed herbage often has a resinous odor. *Aster* is Latin for "star."

Azure Aster

Lindley's Aster (Aster ciliolatus)

Description Common, tall aster of upland forest areas and roadsides, especially in the north. It is usually 2 to 4 feet tall. The lower leaves are elongate, somewhat heart-shaped, and hairless. Margins of lower leaves are toothed. The flower heads, arranged in an elongate cluster, have 10 to 20 blue or purplish rays. *Late summer, autumn*

Habitat and Range Minnesota: mostly in the north; general: northern United States and adjacent Canada.

Azure Aster
(Aster oolentangiensis)

Description A prairie aster, quite similar to the preceding but with lower leaves that have few or no teeth. It is usually 1 to 2 feet tall. *Late summer, autumn*

Habitat and Range Minnesota: prairies, especially in the southeast and center; general: eastern United States.

Blue Wood Aster
(Aster cordifolius)

Description Woodland aster with small blue, lavender, or white flower heads and coarsely toothed, heart-shaped leaves. It is usually 1 to 3 feet tall. Stems are much branched and commonly in clumps. *Late summer, autumn*

Habitat and Range Minnesota: wooded areas, mostly in the south and southeast. It frequently invades shady dooryards and gardens; general: eastern United States.

Comments Also called Heart-leaved Aster.

Blue Wood Aster

New England Aster
(Aster novae-angliae)

Description Robust, hairy aster with deep purple or sometimes rosy flower heads that are 1 to 1½ inches across and have more than 30 narrow rays. Stems, often as tall as 4 feet, are usually clumped and much branched. Bases of the oblong stem leaves clasp the stem. *Autumn*

Habitat and Range Minnesota: common in moist, open places except in the northeast; general: temperate eastern and central North America.

Comments This aster is often grown as a garden perennial. There is also a white variety.

New England Aster

Purple-stemmed Aster

Purple-stemmed Aster
(Aster puniceus)

Description Stout aster of open or brushy wet places. The flower heads, which are 1 to 1½ inches across, have more than 30 pale blue or purplish rays. The stem, commonly 3 to 5 feet tall, is often reddish and has scattered bristly hairs and clasping leaves that are usually toothed. *Autumn*

Habitat and Range Minnesota: throughout in wet places except in the southwest; general: eastern United States.

Smooth Aster
(Aster laevis)

Description A beautiful aster of open or brushy places such as prairie swales and roadsides. It is usually 2 to 4 feet tall and has hairless leaves that clasp the stem. Basal leaves, if present, are not heart-shaped. The flowers are about 1 inch across with 15 to 25 bright blue or blue purple rays. *Autumn*

Habitat and Range Minnesota: throughout, except in the north-east; general: temperate North America.

Comments Smooth Aster is sometimes grown in gardens.

Aromatic Aster
(Aster oblongifolius)

Description Low, much-branched aster of dry prairies. It is usually less than 2 feet tall. Flower heads have rosy purple rays, and beneath these are curved, spreading bracts

Smooth Aster

BILL JOHNSON

Aromatic Aster

that are sticky with aromatic hairs. Stems are brittle, and the oblong, pointed leaves are without stalks. *Autumn*

Habitat and Range Minnesota: dry prairies and open rocky places, mostly in the south; general: eastern and central United States.

RICHARD HAUG

Silky Aster

Silky Aster
(*Aster sericeus*)

Description Low, branched aster of dry, open places. It is usually 1 to 2 feet tall and has small, pointed leaves covered with silky hairs on both sides. The flower heads have rosy purple rays. *Autumn*

Habitat and Range Minnesota: south and west on dry prairies; general: temperate central North America.

Joe-Pye Weed
(Eupatorium maculatum)

Description Robust perennial, usually 3 to 5 feet tall, of swamps and ditch banks. The purplish flower heads are in a flattish cluster. The toothed leaves generally are in whorls of 4 or 5, and the stem is often spotted with purple. *Summer, autumn*

Habitat and Range Minnesota: throughout in moist places; general: temperate North America.

Comments Joe Pye is thought to have been a Native American physician who made use of this plant in New England. Tincture of the roots was used medicinally by early American physicians, and the plant was gathered by the Ojibwe to make "strengthening baths."

Joe-Pye Weed

Sweet Joe-Pye Weed *(Eupatorium purpureum)*

Description Similar to Joe-Pye Weed but with flower heads in a somewhat rounded or domed cluster. Leaves are mostly in whorls of 3 or 4. *Summer, autumn*

Sweet Joe-Pye Weed

RICHARD HAUG

Dotted Blazing Star

Habitat and Range Minnesota: most common in the east and north-central portion, often in thickets and along edges of woods; general: eastern temperate North America.

Dotted Blazing Star
(*Liatris punctata*)

Description Low-growing perennial of prairies. The clumped, erect stems are often less than 1 foot tall and end in a spikelike cluster of purple flower heads. Each head usually has fewer than 8 flowers, and the erect bracts enclosing them are sharply pointed. The narrow leaves are pitted or dotted beneath. *Summer, autumn*

Habitat and Range Minnesota: mostly in the south and west on dry prairies; general: upper Midwest and Great Plains.

Comments The stems of this and the following species usually rise from a thick corm.

Tall Blazing Star
(*Liatris pycnostachya*)

Description Perennial of moist prairies. The unbranched stems are often 3 to 4 feet tall and end in a long spike of small purple flower heads, each with fewer than 8 flowers. The bracts at the base of the flower heads (involucre bracts) are pointed, and the tips curve outward. *Summer, autumn*

Habitat and Range Minnesota: prairies, mostly in the south and west; general: central United States.

Comments This species, including a white variety, is sometimes grown in gardens under the name Kansas Gay Feather.

Tall Blazing Star

Rough Blazing Star

Western Ironweed

Rough Blazing Star
(Liatris aspera)

Description Perennial, usually 1 to 3 feet tall, with unbranched stems ending in a spikelike cluster of purple flower heads. Each head contains more than 15 flowers. The bracts surrounding the flowers are rounded and have a thin, papery margin. *Summer, autumn*

Habitat and Range Minnesota: prairies and open woods, mostly in the south and west; general: temperate eastern North America.

Western Ironweed
(Vernonia fasciculata)

Description Clumped perennial of marshes and wet prairies. It has deep purple flower heads in a spreading cluster. Stems, usually 2 to 4 feet tall, are often reddish, and the elongate leaves are hairless and sharply toothed. *Summer, autumn*

Habitat and Range Minnesota: mostly in the south and west; general: central United States and adjacent Canada.

Comments Western Ironweed often thrives in wet pastures where cattle graze around it.

Canada Thistle
(Cirsium arvense)

Description A common perennial, introduced from Europe, 1 to 5 feet tall, of roadsides, fields, and other open places. Its lobed, spiny-leafed branches bear numerous small purple flower heads. The latter are fragrant and about ½ inch across. Occasionally white. *Summer*

Habitat and Range Minnesota: throughout; general: eastern and central United States.

Comments Bees like them, but gardeners usually do not since the plants spread by underground roots and are difficult to control.

Nodding Thistle
(Carduus nutans)

Description A recent, prickly addition to Minnesota's bouquet of wildflowers. This beautiful Eurasian thistle, a biennial, grows up to 4 feet tall, and has long-stalked purple flower heads 2 to 3 inches across. The flowers are enclosed in spine-tipped bracts, the outermost of which are bent backward. *Summer*

Canada Thistle

Habitat and Range Minnesota: occasional in old fields and prairies in the south, where it is becoming increasingly abundant; general: widely but sparingly distributed in North America.

Comments Nodding Thistle is a non-native species that has become a serious pest in pastures and hayfields.

Nodding Thistle

175

Bull Thistle

Bull Thistle
(*Cirsium vulgare*)

Description A robust, hairy biennial growing to 4 feet or more and having elongate, lobed leaves with crinkled margins and armed with spines. Wings extend down the stem from the base of the leaves. Flower heads are pale purple and often 2 inches or more across. The bracts of the flower head are tipped with stout yellowish spines. *Summer*

Habitat and Range Widely distributed in Minnesota and elsewhere in North America in pastures and waste places and along roads. A native of Eurasia.

Field Thistle
(*Cirsium discolor*)

Description Robust biennial thistle, commonly 3 to 6 feet tall, with elongate, lobed leaves that are nearly flat. The undersurface of the leaves is covered with white hairs, and the margins have weak spines. Flower heads are pale purple, up to 2 inches wide, and have involucre bracts tipped by long, slender spines that stand out at an angle to the heads. *Summer*

Field Thistle

RICHARD HAUG

Swamp Thistle

Habitat and Range Minnesota: dry fields, roadsides, and prairies; general: eastern United States and adjacent Canada.

Swamp Thistle
(Cirsium muticum)

Description Stout biennial thistle, usually 3 to 6 feet tall, of open or brushy swamps. The elongate, lobed leaves are almost flat, green, and nearly hairless when fully grown. Spines on the leaf margins are weak. The wine purple flower heads are about 1½ inches across and have involucre bracts without spines at the tips. *Summer, autumn*

Habitat and Range Minnesota: throughout in swamps except in the south and southwest; general: temperate eastern North America.

Flodman's Thistle
(Cirsium flodmani)

Description Low perennial thistle, usually 1 to 2 feet tall, of prairies, plains, and dry, open places. The elongate stem leaves are cut into spine-tipped lobes, but basal leaves may be without lobes. Leaves are woolly with matted white hairs, at least on the undersurface. The beautiful wine red flower heads are about 2 inches across. *Summer*

Habitat and Range Minnesota: prairies, mostly in the south and west; general: Great Plains.

Blue Lettuce *(Lactuca pulchella)*

Description Perennial, usually 1 to 2 feet tall, of roadsides, prairies, and brushy places. The bright blue

Flodman's Thistle

Blue Lettuce

flower heads, about ¾ inch across, are shaped like those of the dandelion. The elongate, often bluish green leaves are lobed and have milky juice. *Summer*

Habitat and Range Minnesota: throughout but uncommon in the northeast; general: central and western North America.

Chicory (*Cichorium intybus*)

Description Perennial, usually 1 to 3 feet tall, of roadsides and old fields. The bright blue flower heads are 1 to 1½ inches across and set close against the upright stems. (Flower color varies with age and locality and may be almost white, pale blue, or pinkish.) *Summer*

Habitat and Range A Eurasian plant widely distributed in North America.

Comments The thick taproot, when roasted, has long been used as a coffee substitute or additive. The name is very old and of Egyptian or Arabic origin. Also called Blue Sailors.

Rattlesnake-root (*Prenanthes alba*)

Description Perennial of open woods and shady roadsides. It is usually 2 to 3 feet tall and has elongate clusters of nodding flower heads that are white, yellowish, or purple-tinged. Stems and leaves are bluish green. The leaves are stalked, and the leaf blades are variously lobed and often widest toward the base. Bracts of the flower heads are hairless. *Summer*

Habitat and Range Minnesota: throughout, except in the south-

Chicory

west; general: temperate eastern North America.

Glaucous Rattlesnake-root
(*Prenanthes racemosa*)

Description Perennial of prairies. The erect stem, usually 1 to 3 feet tall, ends in a spikelike cluster of purplish flower heads. Each flower head is on a short stalk and directed upward. Bracts of the flower heads are hairy. Leaves are oval to oblong and not lobed. Juice is milky. *Summer*

Habitat and Range Minnesota: mostly in the south and west; general: temperate eastern North America.

SPIDERWORT FAMILY
(*Commelinaceae*)

Asiatic Day Flower
(*Commelina communis*)

Description Low, spreading annual with declining, spreading stems that root at the nodes. Upright stems are usually less than 1 foot tall. Leaves are oblong or oval and pointed. The flowers are about ½ inch across, with 2 blue petals and 1 smaller, white petal. They last only a day. *Summer*

Habitat and Range A native of Asia, widely naturalized in eastern United States in shady places and dooryards.

Rattlesnake-root

Glaucous Rattlesnake-root

WELBY SMITH

Asiatic Day Flower

Comments

The generic name, *Commelina*, which was assigned by Linnaeus, refers to the Commelin brothers, early Dutch botanists, two of whom (the blue petals) were productive botanists, and the third (the white petal), who did little.

Western Spiderwort
(*Tradescantia occidentalis*)

Description Perennial, usually 1 to 2 feet tall, with erect, leafy stems, grasslike leaves, and clustered 3-petaled flowers. Flowers are usually blue but sometimes pink, white, or pale purple. They are about 1¼ inches across, and on hot summer days wilt by noon. The green sepals are sticky with glandular hairs. Herbage is somewhat fleshy and has sticky juice that can be seen as filaments, much like those of a spider web, if segments of a leaf are slowly pulled apart. *Spring, summer*

Habitat and Range Minnesota: open, grassy places mostly in the center and northwest; general: prairies and plains of western North America.

Related Species The Bracted Spiderwort (*Tradescantia bracteata*) is similar, but the sepals are covered with a mixture of soft, normal hairs and hairs tipped by sticky glands.

Lily Family
(*Liliaceae*)

Meadow Garlic
(*Allium canadense*)

Description Low perennial, usually less than 1 foot tall, of

Western Spiderwort

Meadow Garlic

prairies and meadows. The elongate, solid leaves and flowering stems rise from a bulb. Flowers are 6-parted, usually pale purple, and in an umbel. Often, brown bulblets replace some or all of the flowers. *Spring, summer*

Habitat and Range Minnesota: mostly in the south; general: eastern United States.

Comments This and other native onions were used by Native Americans for flavoring. Its Algonquian name, *Shig-gau-ga-whin-zheeg*, means "skunk weed." From it comes *Chicago*, meaning "place where wild onions grow."

Iris Family (*Iridaceae*)

Blue Flag (*Iris versicolor*)

Description Perennial of marshes and shallow water. Leaves are upright, swordlike, and 2-ranked. The branched stem, up to 2 feet tall, bears conspicuous blue flowers that are about 3 inches across. They have 3 spreading, downward-bent sepals and 3 shorter, ascending petals. The fruit is a pod 1½ to 2½ inches long. *Spring, early summer*

Habitat and Range Minnesota: widespread, the common iris in the north; general: upper eastern United States and adjacent Canada.

Comments Rootstocks of blue flags contain emetic and cathartic substances and are poisonous to cattle.

Related Species Shreve's Blue Flag (*Iris virginica* var. *shrevei*) is similar but characterized by larger pods. It is found mostly in southern Minnesota.

Blue Flag

Blue-eyed Grass
(Sisyrinchium montanum)

Description Perennial with grass-like leaves. Commonly tufted and less than 1 foot tall. The violet purple flowers have 6 similar spreading perianth parts. They are usually about ¾ inch across and in a small cluster near the top of the flat, narrow stem. Roots are fibrous. *Spring*

Habitat and Range Minnesota: widespread in open places, often on sandy soil; general: much of temperate North America.

Related Species The Prairie Blue-eyed Grass (*Sisyrinchium campestre*) is similar but has pale blue or white flowers. It is a midwestern species that is widespread in Minnesota.

Blue-eyed Grass

Purple Fringed Orchid

ORCHID FAMILY (*Orchidaceae*)

Purple Fringed Orchid
(Platanthera psycodes)

Description Perennial of damp, open places. The leafy stem is erect, usually 1 to 2 feet tall, and ends in a showy cluster of small purple flowers. These are about ½ inch across. The lip of the flower is 3-lobed and cut into a fringe. *Summer*

Habitat and Range Minnesota: grassy and brushy marshes, mostly in the north and east; general: temperate eastern North America.

Related Species Ten other species of rein orchids are known from Minnesota. All are plants of bogs, marshes, and damp woods, and all have elongate clusters of flowers, each with a spur: the rein. Flowers are greenish, white, or pale yellow. The lip and other flower parts are of the same color, and the lip may or may not be fringed.

Green, Brown, and Maroon
FLOWERS

Alum Root

Saxifrage Family
(*Saxifragaceae*)

Alum Root
(*Heuchera richardsonii*)

Description Perennial of dry prairies and open woods. The stem, usually 1 to 2 feet tall, ends in an elongate cluster of irregularly shaped green or brownish flowers. There is a clump of basal leaves with rounded or heart-shaped blades that are lobed and on hairy stalks. *Summer*

Habitat and Range Minnesota: throughout; general: upper Midwest and Great Plains.

Comments The thick, astringent root was used as a poultice for open sores or wounds.

Birthwort Family
(*Aristolochiaceae*)

Wild Ginger (*Asarum canadense*)

Description Low woodland perennial. It has a pair of hairy, heart- or kidney-shaped leaves at the end of an elongate and rather thick rootstock. The solitary flower is at ground level, between the stalks of the paired leaves. It is dark red or brownish and has 3 triangular calyx lobes. *Spring*

Habitat and Range Minnesota: throughout in hardwood forests; general: temperate eastern North America.

Comments The rootstock has a mild ginger flavor and has been used in Native American and folk medicine.

Wild Ginger

Cashew Family
(*Anacardiaceae*)

Poison Ivy
(*Toxicodendron rydbergii*)

Description Low-growing (4 to 36 inches), woody-stemmed plant having highly variable compound leaves with three leaflets, each about 3 to 4 inches long. They are often shiny, especially in spring, and turn bright yellow or red in the fall. The tiny yellowish or greenish white flowers grow in loose clusters in the leaf axils, often hidden from view. The hard, round, greenish or grayish white fruits, however, are conspicuous in the fall after the leaves have dropped. *Summer*

Poison Ivy

Habitat and Range Minnesota: widespread, except in the extreme northeast corner; general: eastern United States and Canada, south to Mexico. Similar species occur westward. It may also grow as a vine, especially in southeastern Minnesota and in the eastern United States.

Comments Birds eat the fruit with impunity, but every part of the plant, any season, may cause severe inflammation and blistering of the skin in humans. No one is absolutely immune. Crushed leaves and juice of Jewelweed are sometimes used to relieve itching.

Nettle Family (*Urticaceae*)

Stinging Nettle (*Urtica dioica*)

Description Introduced from Europe. A perennial green weed of fields, roadsides, and other open or "waste" places. It grows with unbranched vigor to a height of 4 feet or more. The stem is square, the leaves are stalked, opposite, and somewhat heart-shaped with edges coarsely saw-toothed. From midsummer to fall, clusters of small greenish flowers dangle from the leaf axils. Both the leaves and the stem are covered with stinging hairs. *Summer*

Habitat and Range Minnesota: throughout on moist soils; general: almost cosmopolitan.

Comments Touching Stinging Nettles is like being stung by bees. They are high in nitrogen so make good compost. They are also high in vitamin C and are nutritious for cows as well as humans and can be added to hay or soup for benefits to both.

ASTER FAMILY (*Asteraceae*)

Giant Ragweed (*Ambrosia trifida*)

Description Coarse, weedy annual of waste places, often growing to a height of 6 feet. The opposite leaves are mostly 3-lobed. The flowers differ from most other composites by being wind pollinated. The staminate flower heads, in elongate clusters at the tips of the branches, have copious pollen, a principal cause of hay fever. The female flowers, in the axils of the leaves or bracts, bear small nutlike fruits. *Summer*

Habitat and Range Widely distributed on fertile, disturbed soils in Minnesota and westward.

Comments The fruits are consumed by many seed-eating birds, including pheasants.

Related Species Common Ragweed (*Ambrosia artemisiifolia*) is also a weedy annual but has much-cut leaves and seldom grows taller than 3 feet. The Western Ragweed (*Ambrosia coronopifolia*)

Stinging Nettle

Giant Ragweed

Groundnut

is generally similar but is a perennial with creeping rootstocks. It is most common on dry prairies with sandy soil.

BEAN FAMILY (*Fabaceae*)

Groundnut (*Apios americana*)

Description Perennial twining vine of moist woods, thickets, and stream banks. Leaves are compound, usually with 3 or 5 leaflets. The fragrant brown purple flowers are in rounded clusters. Along the rootstocks are small tubers that were once used for food by Native Americans. It is likely that the plant is spread along streams by tubers washed away during floods. *Summer*

Habitat and Range Minnesota: mostly in the south; general: temperate eastern North America.

Comments The tubers were eaten by the Pilgrims during their first winter in New England. Groundnut was early taken to Europe as a prospective crop plant. It was found, however, that several years were required to produce a sizable crop of tubers.

Pineapple-weed (*Chamomilla suaveolens*)

Description Low, weedy annual, usually less than 6 inches tall. The small flower heads are greenish and without rays. Leaves are much divided and when crushed, have a pineapple odor. Patches of Pineapple-weed also give off this odor after a rain. *Summer*

Pineapple-weed

Prairie Sage

Habitat and Range A native of the western United States, it has become naturalized in eastern North America and Europe. It grows throughout Minnesota, often in dooryards and along driveways.

Comments Pineapple-weed thrives in areas grazed by geese and ducks, such as around Silver Lake, Rochester, Minnesota. We have also seen it growing in goose pens in northern England.

Prairie Sage
(*Artemisia ludoviciana*)

Description Erect perennial, usually 1 to 2 feet tall, with leaves covered on both sides with soft white hairs. The leaves are usually without teeth and have an aromatic sagebrush odor when crushed. The small grayish flower heads are in an elongate, pyramidal cluster. *Autumn*

Habitat and Range Minnesota: prairies and pastures mostly in the south and west, often growing in patches; general: western North America.

Comments Also called Western Mugwort.

Related Species The Saw-tooth White Sage (*Artemisia serrata*) is similar but has coarsely toothed leaves that are green above and white beneath. It is a midwestern species growing in open, grassy places, usually on moister sites than the Prairie Sage.

Common Wormwood
(*Artemisia absinthium*)

Description Robust perennial, usually 1 to 3 feet tall, with much divided leaves that are very aro-

EVELYN MOYLE

Common Wormwood

matic and gray with soft, silky hairs. The small gray flower heads are in an elongate, somewhat leafy cluster. *Summer*

Habitat and Range Minnesota: dry fields, roadsides, and waste places. It thrives in overgrazed pastures; general: a European species that is widely naturalized in temperate North America.

Comments In Europe it was once an ingredient in the habit-forming liqueur absinthe, a use now outlawed in most countries. Also called Absinth and Mugwort.

Cattail Family (*Typhaceae*)

Narrow-leaved Cattail
(*Typha angustifolia*)

Description Clumped perennial, often 6 feet or more tall, of marshes, shores, and shallow water. Leaves are elongate, about ½ inch wide, and the minute flowers are in a dense spike. In this species the lower (pistillate) portion of the spike is separated from the upper

Narrow-leaved Cattail

(staminate) portion by a stretch of smooth stem. The staminate flowers fall soon after shedding pollen, leaving only rough stem. Seeds are wind-borne on a tuft of down. *Summer*

Habitat and Range Minnesota: throughout but not common in the northeast; general: northern and eastern United States and adjacent Canada. This species has become increasingly abundant in Minnesota since the 1930s.

Related Species The Common Cattail (*Typha latifolia*) is shorter, has wider leaves, and has no gap between the staminate and pistillate parts of the spike. Widely distributed and common.

Grass Family (*Poaceae*)

Wild Rice (*Zizania palustris*)

Description Grows in shallow waters of lakes and streams and usually stands 3 to 6 feet tall when mature. The ribbonlike leaves are at first submerged and then float. In summer the stem emerges from the water, and flowers. By early autumn the grains ripen. *Summer, early autumn*

Habitat and Range Minnesota: common in the north, where there are 30,000 acres in wild, self-seeding stands; general: Great Lakes region and southern Manitoba. Occasional elsewhere. Frequently planted as a waterfowl food plant.

Comments This aquatic grass remains a staple food of the Ojibwe. The grains are harvested by knocking them into a canoe with short hand flails and then processed by parching and removing the husks. Wild Rice is also grown domestically in paddies and is widely used as a gourmet food.

Wild Rice

ARUM FAMILY (*Araceae*)

Jack-in-the-pulpit

Jack-in-the-pulpit
(*Arisaema triphyllum*)

Description Erect, often reddish perennial of moist woods. Usually about 1 foot tall. Leaves are compound with 3 pointed leaflets. The small flowers are crowded near the base of a clublike spadix (Jack) that is enclosed in a narrow, funnel-shaped structure (spathe) that has an overhanging flap at the top, the old-style "pulpit." In late summer a cluster of bright red berries is exposed by the withering of the spathe. *Spring, summer*

Habitat and Range Minnesota: throughout; general: temperate eastern North America.

Comments The thickened root (corm) at the base of the plant, and to a lesser extent other plant parts, contains needlelike calcium oxalate crystals, which cause a burning sensation if eaten. Also called Indian Turnip.

Skunk Cabbage
(*Symplocarpus foetidus*)

Description Among the first wildflowers of spring, and the oddest. The pointed, brown or purplish spathe, 4 to 6 inches high, encloses a club-like stem, the spadix, on which are tiny flowers. Pollinating insects enter this botanical tepee, prob-ably attracted by odor, warmth, and shelter. Later the fruit, much like a small-stalked and roughened potato, develops beneath the clump of very large summer leaves. The fruit contains large, acrid seeds in a bland pulp. The entire plant has a skunky odor. *Spring*

Skunk Cabbage

RICHARD HAUG

Habitat and Range Minnesota: along the eastern border in swamps and seepage areas; general: temperate eastern North America. Also in Asia.

Sweet Flag (*Acorus calamus*)

Description Clumped perennial of marshes and shallow water. Usually 2 to 4 feet tall. Its erect, swordlike leaves are much like those of Blue Flag, except they are yellowish green, rather than bluish green, and aromatic. The small flowers, and later the dried fruits, are in a dense cluster (spadix) near the top of the flattened, leaflike stem. The spathe, conspicuous in many members of the arum family, in

Sweet Flag

EVELYN MOYLE

Northern Bog-orchid

Sweet Flag is the tapering upper part of the stem. *Summer*

Habitat and Range Minnesota: throughout, often in and along streams; general: temperate North America. Also in Eurasia.

Comments Sweet Flag has had considerable use in Native American and folk medicine. In pioneer times the rootstocks were thinly sliced and candied. However, some strains may contain a carcinogen.

ORCHID FAMILY (*Orchidaceae*)

Northern Bog-orchid
(*Platanthera hyperborea*)

Description A common leafy-stemmed orchid, 8 inches to about 3 feet in height, topped by dense spikes of small green or yellowish green flowers. The small flowers are slightly hooded with in-curved top and side petals. The petals are narrow and plain (no bumps or fringes); the lip and spur are about equal in length, but the spur is slightly curved. The flowers are fragrant and may be pollinated by mosquitoes. *Spring, summer*

Habitat and Range Minnesota: throughout, but uncommon in south and west; general: Arctic North America from Alaska to Greenland south to Pennsylvania and southern borders of the Great Lakes, northwest to the Pacific Coast. It apparently is not fussy as to soils, growing in many moist places—shores, swamps, marshes, thickets in sun or shade, and often abundantly.

Comments Also called Northern Green Orchid.

🌸 *Glossary*

achene A dry, seedlike fruit.

acrid Having a sharp burning or biting taste.

alternate With a single leaf at a stem node.

annual Completes life cycle in 1 year.

anther The pollen-bearing part of a stamen.

arching With tip bent backward or outward.

ascending Rising upward at an angle, obliquely.

awn A bristlelike structure, especially on a grass spikelet.

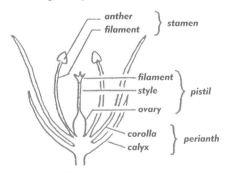

Flower in sectional view

axil The inside angle of the junction of leaf and stem.

balsamic A sweet, aromatic, somewhat resinous odor.

basal Rising directly from underground parts; usually refers to leaves.

biennial Completes life cycle in 2 years.

blade The part of a leaf or leaflet above the stalk.

bract A small, leaflike structure below a flower; *see also* involucre.

bulb A short, underground stem covered with scaly leaves; like an onion.

calyx The outermost or lowermost series of flower parts, often green; made up of sepals.

capsule A dry fruit containing seeds; a pod.

clasping Referring to a leaf base that goes all or partly around the stem.

compound Having several similar parts or arrangements, as a compound leaf with leaflets or a compound umbel.

corm The thick, underground portion

of a stem, usually rounded and often somewhat flattened.

corolla The series of flower parts second from the bottom or the outside of a flower; usually colored; made up of petals.

cultivar A variety of plant selected by horticulturists; usually not persisting in the wild.

cut Refers to leaves with margins deeply divided into narrow, often irregular segments.

disk The central portion of some flower heads, such as sunflowers and asters; may be flat or raised.

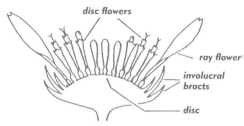

disc flowers

ray flower

involucral bracts

disc

Diagram of a typical composite head, in sectional view

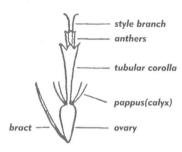

style branch

anthers

tubular corolla

pappus(calyx)

bract

ovary

Disk flower of composite

divided Separated into distinct, often narrow segments, as in some leaves.

filament The stalk of a stamen, usually slender.

flower head *See* head.

follicle An elongate pod opening along one edge to release seeds.

free Not attached to other parts.

fruit Seed or seeds with attached or enclosing parts; may be dry or fleshy.

fused With parts grown together.

glabrous Without hairs.

gland A cell filled with resin, oil, or other substance; may be stalked or make a semitransparent or dark dot in the leaf blade.

haustorium An elongate structure, usually short and somewhat rootlike, whereby a parasitic plant penetrates the stems of other plants. (See description of Dodder for an example.)

head A compact inflorescence of essentially stalkless flowers.

herbage Stems and leaves considered together.

inflorescence The flowering part of a plant.

involucre Applied to a head in the composite family (Compositae); a series of reduced leaves (bracts) enclosing or surrounding the flowers in the head.

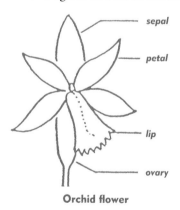

sepal

petal

lip

ovary

Orchid flower

irregular Flower parts other than regular; *see* regular. Includes flowers with 2 lips, bilateral symmetry, spurs, or parts of markedly different sizes or with nonsymmetrical arrangements.

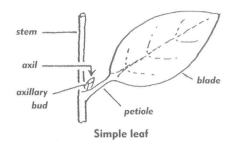

Simple leaf

leaflet One of the like parts of a compound leaf; the leaflets are attached to the central axis of the leaf or to the end of the petiole, not to the stem.

lip The enlarged or otherwise modified outer portion of 1 of the petals, especially in the Orchidaceae.

lobed In leaves, the wide divisions of the margin, extending more than halfway to the center of the blade.

midrib The central vein of a pinnately veined leaf.

nerves The principal veins running the length of a leaf blade; counts of nerves may include the midrib, as in 3-nerved.

node The stem joint, sometimes swollen, at which leaves may rise.

opposite With two leaves at a node; paired.

ovary The enlarged, basal part of the pistil that encloses the ovules.

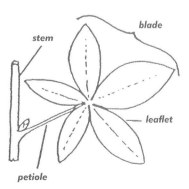

Palmately compound leaf

ovule The female structure in the pistil that after fertilization becomes a seed.

palmate In a spreading pattern, like fingers on a hand; refers to leaf venation and lobing.

panicle A loose inflorescence, like the spikelets of grasses.

pappus The modified calyx of the compositae in which the sepals have been modified into awns, scales, or bristles.

parallel Referring to leaf venation; veins running side by side the length of the leaf blade, as in a grass leaf.

Pinnately compound leaf

perennial A plant whose life cycle may span 3 years or more.

perianth The outer, similar flower parts considered together; may be sepals or both sepals and petals.

petal A segment of the corolla (*see* corolla); may be separate or fused to other petals.

petiole The stalk of a leaf; not always present.

pinnate A featherlike arrangement with side branches or divisions extending along a central, elongate axis.

pistil Seed-bearing organ of the flower, consisting usually of ovary, stigma, and style.

raceme An elongate inflorescence on

which individual flowers are distinctly stalked; *see also* spike.

rank The arrangement of leaves on a stem or in a basal tuft; in a 2-ranked pattern the leaves are all on one plane.

ray or ray flower In the composite family (Compositae), the flattened or strap-like flowers on the edge of a head; often petal-like.

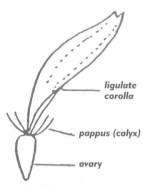

ligulate corolla

pappus (calyx)

ovary

Ray flower of composite

regular As applied to a flower, one that is radially symmetrical in shape. Perianth parts are all similar in size, shape, and arrangement. Includes wheel-, cup-, vase-, and tube-shaped flowers.

rhizome *See* rootstock.

rootstock An underground stem, often growing parallel to the ground surface.

rosette A spreading, flat-lying cluster of basal leaves.

sepal A segment of the calyx (*see* calyx); often green but may be colored; frequently small or falling early.

spadix A dense, often fleshy spike characteristic of the arum family (Araceae); on it small flowers are crowded.

spathe A leaflike or funnel-like structure enclosing or associated with a spadix.

spike An elongate inflorescence bearing flowers or flower heads that are essentially stalkless.

spikelet A scaly or chaffy inflorescence, such as in grasses; a small spike.

spur A saclike or tubelike flower structure, often part of a petal or sepal and containing nectar.

stamen A slender male flower structure bearing pollen; the third series of flower parts from the bottom or outside of the flower.

stem The axis of the plant to which the leaves and flowers are attached.

stigma The part of the pistil that is specialized for the reception of pollen, usually distinguished by its sticky or minutely granular surface.

stipule A leaflike structure borne in pairs at the base of the leaf stalk of some kinds of plants; may be free or fused and collarlike.

style In many pistils, the prolonged, sometimes slender upper portion that separates the stigma from the ovary; not always present.

taproot A root, usually unbranched and growing downward; like a carrot.

tendril A slender, twining structure of a climbing plant; usually a modified leaf or leaflet.

tuber The enlarged end of an underground stem, usually rounded and fleshy, in which food is stored.

umbel A cluster of stalked flowers, all of which rise at about the same place, like spokes in an umbrella.

whorl A cluster of 3 or more leaves growing at the same stem node.

✿ Bibliography

Aiken, George D. 1994. *Pioneering with Wild Flowers*. Brattleboro, Vt.: Alan C. Hood and Company.

Chadde, Steve. 1998. *A Great Lakes Wetland Flora: A Complete, Illustrated Guide to the Aquatic and Wetland Plants of the Upper Midwest*. Calumet, Mich.: PocketFlora Press.

Courtenay, Booth, and James H. Zimmerman. 1972. *Wildflowers and Weeds*. New York: Van Nostrand Reinhold.

Curtis, John T. 1992. *The Vegetation of Wisconsin: An Ordination of Plant Communities*. Madison: University of Wisconsin Press.

Densmore, Frances. 1974. *How Indians Use Wild Plants for Food, Medicine, and Crafts*. New York: Dover Publications.

Eggers, Steve D., and Donald M. Reed. 1997. *Wetland Plants and Plant Communities of Minnesota and Wisconsin*. St. Paul: U.S. Army Corps of Engineers, St. Paul District.

Fernald, Merritt L., Alfred C. Kinsey, and Reed C. Rollins. 1996. *Edible Wild Plants of Eastern North America*. New York: Dover Publications.

Foster, Steven, and James A. Duke. 1999.

A Field Guide to Medicinal Plants and Herbs of Eastern and Central North America. 3d ed. Boston: Houghton Mifflin Co.

Gleason, H. A., and A. Cronquist. 1991. *Manual of Vascular Plants of Northeastern United States and Adjacent Canada*. 2d ed. New York: New York Botanical Garden.

Great Plains Flora Association. 1986. *Flora of the Great Plains*. Lawrence: University Press of Kansas.

Ladd, Doug. 1995. *Tallgrass Prairie Wildflowers*. Helena, Mont.: Falcon Press.

Lakela, Olga. 1965. *Flora of Northeastern Minnesota*. Minneapolis: University of Minnesota Press.

Minnesota Department of Natural Resources. 1999. *A Guide to Minnesota's Scientific and Natural Areas*. St. Paul: Section of Wildlife, Scientific and Natural Areas Program, Minnesota Department of Natural Resources.

Minnesota Native Plant Society. 1996. *Minnesota Native Plant Society's Guide to Spring Wildflowers: Twin Cities Region*. St. Paul: Minnesota Native Plant Society, University of Minnesota.

Morley, Thomas. 1969. *Spring Flora of Minnesota: Including Common Cultivated Plants*. Minneapolis: University of Minnesota Press.

Muenscher, Walter Conrad Leopold. 1962. *Poisonous Plants of the United States*. Rev. ed. New York: Macmillan.

Nature Conservancy, The. 1994. *The Guide to The Nature Conservancy Preserves in Minnesota*. Minneapolis: The Nature Conservancy, Minnesota Chapter.

Newcomb, Lawrence. 1977. *Newcomb's Wildflower Guide: An Ingenious New Key System for Quick, Positive Field Identification of the Wildflowers, Flowering Shrubs and Vines of Northeastern and North Central America*. Boston: Little, Brown and Company.

Ownbey, Gerald B. 1971. *Common Wildflowers of Minnesota*. Minneapolis: University of Minnesota Press.

Ownbey, Gerald B., and Thomas Morley. 1991. *Vascular Plants of Minnesota: A Checklist and Atlas*. Minneapolis: University of Minnesota Press.

Peterson, Roger Tory, and Margaret McKenny. 1998. *A Field Guide to Wildflowers: Northeastern and North Central America*. Rev. ed. Boston: Houghton Mifflin Company.

Smith, Welby R. 1993. *Orchids of Minnesota*. Minneapolis: University of Minnesota Press.

Stensaas, Mark. 1996. *Canoe Country Flora: Plants and Trees of the North Woods and Boundary Waters*. Duluth: Pfeifer-Hamilton.

Stokes, Donald, and Lillian Stokes. 1992. *The Wildflower Book: East of the Rockies: An Easy Guide to Growing and Identifying Wildflowers*. Boston: Little, Brown and Co.

Vance, Fenton R., James R. Jowsey, James S. McLean, and Francis A. Switzer. 1999. *Wildflowers of the Northern Great Plains*. 3d ed. Minneapolis: University of Minnesota Press.

✿ Index

The late **John B. Moyle** was a biologist and research supervisor at the Minnesota Department of Natural Resources and a frequent contributor to the *Minnesota Conservation Volunteer*. **Evelyn W. Moyle** is a longtime wildflower enthusiast, photographer, and gardener. She lectures and leads wildflower walks near her home in Excelsior, Minnesota.

John Gregor, owner of ColdSnap Photography, specializes in garden and nature photography and is a regular contributor to *Minnesota Monthly*, *Midwest Home and Garden*, and the *Minnesota Conservation Volunteer*. He is the photographer of *Growing Home: Stories of Ethnic Gardening* by Susan Davis Price (Minnesota, 2000).